THROUGH THE YEAR WITH WESLEY

THROUGH THE YEAR WITH WESLEY

An Anthology

COMPILED AND EDITED BY

Frederick C. Gill

THE UPPER ROOM
Nashville, Tennessee

THROUGH THE YEAR WITH WESLEY

Cover transparency is of a portrait of John Wesley by Frank Salisbury. The original of this painting hangs in the museum of the World Methodist Council, Lake Junaluska, North Carolina.

Cover Design: Linda Bryant
Book Design: Harriette Bateman

First Printing by The Upper Room: November 1983 (7)
Library of Congress Catalog Card Number: 83-50522
ISBN 0-8358-0469-0

Contents

Introduction

by Maxie D. Dunnam

I am a United Methodist by deliberate choice. I was reared in another domination, and my conversion and initial growth in discipleship occurred there. In the past ten years, writings from the Roman Catholic tradition have nurtured me, and some of the most significant persons in my life have been Roman Catholics. I do believe I am ecumenical in experience and perspective.

At the same time, I am an avid United Methodist, and with great enthusiasm I claim John Wesley as a hero.

When I was sixteen years old, I began to sense God treating me in what I thought was a special way. Gradually it became clear that God was calling me to preach. Without talking about this to anyone, I decided I must explore different faith expressions. If I ever answered the call to preach, I wanted to be in what for me was the "right" denomination. Choosing a church had not been deliberate in the past; now it would be, in light of the fact that I vaguely knew I would be spending my vocational life in a particular denomination.

It was then that I met John Wesley. In looking at the history, theological emphasis, and polity of different denominations, I was drawn to John Wesley and then to the church that is his legacy to the world.

So it pleases me to write this introduction to *Through the Year with Wesley*. I confess that I discovered this book only two years ago. Though the book was originally published in London in

7

1954 when I was serving my first charge as a local Methodist preacher, I had missed it. When I was World Editor of The Upper Room, we looked for devotional literature, especially for works which would enhance the celebration of Methodism's bicentennial in the United States. It was then that the curator of the museum at Wesley Chapel in London called this book to my attention.

What a rich discovery! And what a way to appropriate the best of John Wesley: a reading each day for one year. This is a devotional book in the truest sense. That being the case, we need to heed a warning from Wesley:

> Do not imagine an outward form, a round of duties, is religion. Do not suppose that honesty, justice and whatever is called morality (though excellent in its place) is religion. And least of all dream that orthodoxy, right opinion, vulgarly called faith, is religion.

We have not been "religious" and responded to God's daily call upon our life simply because we spend some time each day reading the Bible, these sayings of Wesley, and praying. Only as we express in our daily action, attitudes, and relationships what we discover in the Bible, in these writings of Wesley, and in prayer, will our daily devotional time be fruitful and life-changing.

And it can be life-changing. In these readings is the heartbeat of one of history's most significant Christian leaders. Wesley believed that the union of knowledge and vital piety was a desperate need. He also felt that the dual emphasis—love of God and love of others—was the heart of the Christian faith.

As I think of this volume being published during the bicentennial year of American Methodism, I recall the first conference in the United States—in Baltimore, Christmas, 1784. The question was asked, "What can we rightfully expect as the task of Methodists in America?" The answer was clear: to reform a continent and spread scriptural holiness across the land.

Wesley was pleased with that, and he would be pleased today if this volume would assist us in reclaiming and performing that task. I pray that you will use this volume to that end.

JANUARY

1

First let us agree what religion is. I take religion to be, not the bare saying over so many prayers, morning and evening, in public or in private; not anything superadded now and then to a careless or worldly life; but a constant ruling habit of soul, a renewal of our minds in the image of God, a recovery of the Divine likeness, a still-increasing conformity of heart and life to the pattern of our most holy Redeemer. But if this be religion, if this be that way to life which our blessed Lord hath marked out for us, how can any one, while he keeps close to this way, be charged with running into extremes?

TO RICHARD MORGAN, 1734

2

It is the glory of the people called Methodists that they condemn none for their opinions or modes of worship. They think and let think, and insist upon nothing but faith working by love.

TO MRS HOWTON, 1783

The Methodists are to spread life among all denominations.

TO THOMAS TAYLOR, 1790

I care not a rush for your being called a Papist or Protestant. But I am grieved at your being a heathen. Certain it is that the general religion both of Protestants and Catholics is no better than refined heathenism.

TO HIS NEPHEW, SAMUEL WESLEY, 1790

3

Do not imagine an outward form, a round of duties, is religion. Do not suppose that honesty, justice and whatever is called morality (though excellent in its place) is religion. And least of all dream that orthodoxy, right opinion, vulgarly called faith, is religion.

THE END OF CHRIST'S COMING

Without zeal it is impossible either to make any considerable progress in religion ourselves or to do any considerable service to our neighbour.

ZEAL

Whoever trusts in himself will be confounded.

REDEEMING THE TIME

4

At this season we usually distribute coals and bread among the poor of the Society; but I now considered they wanted clothes as well as food. So on this and the four following days I walked through the town and begged two hundred pounds, in order to clothe them that wanted it most. But it was hard work, as most of the streets were filled with melting snow, which often lay ankle-deep, so that my feet were steeped in snow-water from morning till evening. I held it out pretty well till Saturday evening, when I was laid up with a violent flux.

JOURNAL, 4th JANUARY 1785

5

We do not place the whole of religion (as too many do, God knoweth) either in doing no harm or in doing good or in using the ordinances of God. No, not in all of them together; wherein we know by experience a man may labour many years, and at the end have no true religion at all, no more than he had at the beginning. Much less in any one of these; or, it may be, in a scrap of one of them: Like her who fancies herself a virtuous woman, only because she is not a prostitute; or him who dreams he is an honest man, merely because he does not rob or steal. May the Lord God of my fathers preserve me from such a poor, starved religion as this!

THE CHARACTER OF A METHODIST

6

A Methodist is one who has the love of God shed abroad in his heart by the Holy Ghost given unto him, one who loves the Lord his God with all his heart, and with all his soul, and with all his mind, and with all his strength. God is the joy of his heart and the desire of his soul, which is constantly crying out: 'Whom have I in heaven but Thee? and there is none upon earth that I desire beside Thee! My God and my all! Thou art the strength of my heart and my portion for ever!'

THE CHARACTER OF A METHODIST

7

By these marks, by these fruits of a living faith, do we labour to distinguish ourselves from the unbelieving world, from all those whose minds or lives are not according to the Gospel of Christ. But from real Christians, of whatever denomination they be, we earnestly desire not to be distinguished at all; not from any who sincerely follow after what they know they have not yet attained. No: 'Whosoever doeth the will of my Father which is in heaven, the same is my brother and sister and mother.' And I beseech you, brethren, by the mercies of God, that we be in no wise divided among ourselves.

THE CHARACTER OF A METHODIST

8

Hear ye this, all ye that are called Methodists. You constantly speak of salvation by faith, and you are right in so doing.... But consider, meantime, that let us have ever so much faith, and be our faith ever so strong, it will never save us from hell, unless it now save us from all unholy tempers; from pride, passion, impatience; from all arrogance of spirit, all haughtiness and overbearing; from wrath, anger, bitterness; from discontent, murmuring, fretfulness, peevishness. We are of all men most inexcusable, if having been so frequently guarded against that strong delusion, we still, while we indulge any of these tempers, bless ourselves and dream we are in the way to heaven.

CHARITY

9

Observe all the time the greatest exactness in your regimen or manner of living. Abstain from all mixed or high-seasoned food. Use plain diet easy of digestion, and this as sparingly as you can consistent with ease and strength. Drink only water if it agrees with your stomach, if not, good clear small beer. Use as much exercise daily in the open air as you can, without weariness. Sup at six or seven on the lightest food; go to bed early, and rise betimes. To preserve with steadiness in this course is often more than half the cure. Above all, add to the rest, for it is not labour lost, that old-fashioned medicine—prayer; and have faith in God.

PRIMITIVE PHYSIC

10

The passions have a greater influence upon health than most people are aware of. All violent and sudden passions dispose to or actually throw people into acute diseases. Till the passion which caused the disease is calmed, medicine is applied in vain.

The love of God, as it is the sovereign remedy of all miseries, so in particular it effectually prevents all the bodily disorders the passions introduce, by keeping the passions themselves within due bounds; and by the unspeakable calm serenity and tranquillity it gives the mind, it becomes the most powerful of all the means of health and long life.

PRIMITIVE PHYSIC

11

A drunkard is a public enemy.

A WORD TO A DRUNKARD

You are an enemy to yourself, you throw away your own blessing, if you neglect to keep the Sabbath day holy.

A WORD TO A SABBATH BREAKER

Distilled liquors have their use, but are infinitely overbalanced by the abuse of them; therefore, were it in my power, I would banish them out of the world.

TO THOMAS WRIDE, 1787

12

I myself find more life in the Church prayers than in any formal extemporary prayers of Dissenters. Nay, I find more profit in sermons on either good temper or good works than in what are vulgarly called Gospel sermons. That term is now become a mere cant word; I wish none of our Society would use it. It has no determinate meaning. Let but a pert, selfsufficient animal, that has neither grace nor sense, bawl out something about Christ and his blood or justification by faith, and his hearers cry out: 'What a fine Gospel sermon!' Surely the Methodists have not so learned Christ! We know no Gospel without salvation from sin.

TO MARY BISHOP, 1778

13

Go and see the poor and sick in their own poor little hovels. Take up your cross, woman! Remember the faith! Jesus went before you and will go with you. Put off the gentlewoman; you bear a higher character.

.   .   .   .   .

I have found some of the uneducated poor who have exquisite taste and sentiment; and many, very many, of the rich who have scarcely any at all.

.   .   .   .   .

Beware of indulging gloomy thoughts; they are the bane of thankfulness. You are encompassed with ten thousand mercies; let these sink you into humble thankfulness.

TO MISS MARCH, 1775-7

14

Always remember the essence of Christian holiness is simplicity and purity: one design, one desire: entire devotion to God.

.   .   .   .   .

To use the grace given is the certain way to obtain more grace. To use all the faith you have will bring an increase of faith.

. . . . .

The dealings of God with man are infinitely varied and cannot be confined to any general rule.

. . . . .

Pray, just as you are led, without reasoning, in all simplicity. Be a little child, hanging on him that loves you.

TO MISS MARCH 1770-2

15

I am content with whatever entertainment I meet with, and my companions are always in good humour. . . . This must be the spirit of all who take journeys with me. If a dinner ill-dressed, or hard bed, a poor room, a shower of rain, or a dusty road will put them out of humour, it lays a burden upon me greater than all the rest put together. By the grace of God I never fret, I repine at nothing. I am discontented with nothing. And to hear persons at my ear fretting and murmuring at everything is like tearing the flesh off my bones.

TO EBENEZER BLACKWELL, 1755

We are really a company of poor gentlemen! But we have food and raiment and content.

TO CHRISTOPHER HOPPER, 1774

16

I have again and again, with all the plainness I could, declared what our constant doctrines are, whereby we are distinguished only from heathens or nominal Christians, not from any that worship God in spirit and in truth. Our main doctrines, which include all the rest, are three—that of Repentance, of Faith and of Holiness. The first of these we account, as it were, the porch of religion; the next, the door; the third, religion itself.

TO THOMAS CHURCH, 1746

17

But it was not long before the stewards found a great difficulty with regard to the sick. . . . When I was apprised of this, I laid the case at large before the whole Society; showed how impossible it was for the stewards to attend all that were sick in all parts of the town; desired the leaders of classes would more carefully enquire, and more constantly inform them, who were sick; and asked, 'Who among you is willing as well as able to supply this lack of service?'

The next morning many willingly offered themselves. I chose six and forty of them, divided the town into twenty-three parts, and desired two of them to visit the sick in each division.

TO THE REV. VINCENT PERRONET, 1748

18

But I was still in pain for many of the poor that were sick; there was so great expense, and so little profit. . . . At length I thought of a kind of desperate expedient. I will prepare and give them physic myself.' For seven and twenty years I had made anatomy and physic the diversion of my leisure hours, though I never properly studied them, unless for a few months when I was going to America, where I imagined I might be of some service to those who had no regular physician among them. I applied to it again. I took into my assistance an apothecary and experienced surgeon; resolving at the same time not to go out of my depth but to leave

all difficult and complicated cases to such physicians as the
patients should choose.

TO THE REV. VINCENT PERRONET, 1748

19

I gave notice of this[1] to the Society; telling them that all who
were ill of chronical distempers (for I did not care to venture
upon acute) might, if they pleased, come to me at such a time,
and I would give them the best advice I could and the best
medicines I had.

Many came (and so every Friday since); among the rest was
one William Kirkman, a weaver, near Old Nichol Street. I asked
him: 'What complaint have you?' 'Oh sir,' said he, 'a cough, a
very sore cough. I can get no rest day nor night.'

I asked: 'How long have you had it?' He replied: 'About
threescore years; it began when I was eleven years old.' I was
nothing glad that this man should come first, fearing our not
curing him might discourage others. However, I looked up to
God, and said: 'Take this three or four times a day. If it does you
no good, it will do you no harm.' He took it two or three days.
His cough was cured, and has not returned to this day.

TO THE REV. VINCENT PERRONET, 1748

20

To each of those of whose seriousness and good conversation I
found no reason to doubt I gave a testimony under my own hand
by writing their name on a ticket prepared for that purpose,
every ticket implying as strong a recommendation of the person
to whom it was given as if I had wrote at length: 'I believe the
bearer hereof to be one that fears God and works righteousness.'

[1]That is, his decision to treat simple cases of sickness.

Those who bore these tickets (these σύμβολα or *tesserae,* as the ancients termed them, being of just the same force with the commendatory letters', mentioned by the Apostle), wherever they came, were acknowledged by their brethren and received with all cheerfulness.

TO THE REV. VINCENT PERRONET, 1748

21

'Are you going to hear Mr Wesley?' said a friend to Mr Blackwell. 'No,' he answered; 'I am going to hear God. I listen to *him,* whoever preaches, otherwise I lose all my labour.'

TO MISS MARCH, 1776

I go to Church whether the minister is good or bad, and advise others so to do.

TO JAMES REA, 1766

Unstable Methodists will always be subject to the temptation of sermon-hunting.

TO THOMAS TAYLOR, 1791

22

If anyone desire to know exactly what quantity of sleep his own constitution requires, he may very easily make the experiment which I made about sixty years ago; I then waked every night about twelve or one, and lay awake for some time. I readily concluded that this arose from my lying longer in bed than nature required. To be satisfied, I procured an alarum, which waked me the next morning at seven, (nearly an hour earlier than I rose the day before,) yet I lay awake again at night. The second morning I rose at six; but notwithstanding this, I lay awake the second night. The third morning I rose at five; but nevertheless I lay awake the third night. The fourth morning I rose at four, (as, by the grace of God, I have done ever since). And I lay awake no more.

REDEEMING THE TIME

23

As for me, I never think of my style at all, but just set down the words that come first. Only when I transcribe anything for the press, then I think it my duty to see that every phrase be clear, pure and proper. Conciseness (which is now as it were natural to me) brings *quantum sufficit* of strength. If, after all, I observe any stiff expression, I throw it out, neck and shoulders. Clearness in particular is necessary for you and me, because we are to instruct people of the least understanding.

A GOOD STYLE

24

I went to America to convert the Indians; but, O! who shall convert me? who, what is he that will deliver me from this evil heart of unbelief? I have a fair summer religion. I can talk well; nay, and believe myself, while no danger is near: but let death look me in the face, and my spirit is troubled.

It is now two years and almost four months since I left my native country, in order to teach the Georgian Indians the nature of Christianity; but what have I learned myself in the meantime? Why, (what I the least of all suspected), that I who went to America to convert others, was never myself converted to God.[1] I am not mad, though I thus speak; but I speak the words of truth and soberness.

JOURNAL, 24th-29th JANUARY 1738

[1] I am not sure of this (Wesley's own note).

25

At noon our third storm began. . . . The winds roared round about us, and (what I have never heard before) whistled as distinctly as if it had been a human voice. The ship not only rocked to and fro with the utmost violence, but shook and jarred with so unequal, grating a motion that one could not but with great difficulty keep one's hold of anything, nor stand for a moment without it. Every ten minutes came a shock against the stern or side of the ship, which one would think should dash the planks in pieces. At this time a child, privately baptized before, was brought to be received into the Church. It put me in mind of Jeremiah's buying the field, when the Chaldeans were on the point of destroying Jerusalem, and seemed a pledge of the mercy God designed to shew us, even in the land of the living.

JOURNAL, 25th JANUARY 1736

26

What is it that constitutes *a good style*? Perspicuity and purity, propriety, strength, and easiness, joined together. Where any one of these is wanting, it is not a good style. Dr Middleton's style wants easiness: it is *stiff* to a high degree. And stiffness in writing is full as great a fault as stiffness in behaviour. It is a blemish hardly to be excused, much less to be imitated. He is *pedantic*. 'It is pedantry,' says the great Lord Boyle, 'to use a hard word where an easier will serve.'

TO THE REV. SAMUEL FURLY, 1764

27

If you imitate any writer, let it be South, Atterbury or Swift, in whom *all* the properties of a good writer meet. I was myself once much fonder of Prior than Pope; as I did not then know that stiffness was a fault. But what in all Prior can equal, for beauty of style, some of the first lines that Pope ever published?...

Here is style! How clear, how pure, proper, strong, and yet how amazingly easy! This crowns all; no stiffness, no hard words; no *apparent* art, no affectation; all is natural, and therefore consummately beautiful. Go thou and *write* likewise.

TO THE REV. SAMUEL FURLY, 1764

28

When I had been a member of the University about ten years, I wrote and talked much as you do now. But when I talked to plain people in the Castle or the town, I observed they gaped and stared. This quickly obliged me to alter my style and adopt the language of those I spoke to. And yet there is a dignity in this simplicity, which is not disagreeable to those of the highest rank.... You are a Christian minister, speaking and writing to save souls. Have this end always in your eye, and you will never designedly use a hard word. Use all the sense, learning and fire you have; forgetting yourself, and remembering only these are the souls for whom Christ died.

TO THE REV. SAMUEL FURLY, 1764

29

This, then, have I learned in the ends of the earth, that I am fallen short of the glory of God....

If it be said that I have faith.... so the Apostles had even at Cana in Galilee, when Jesus first manifested forth his glory; even then they, in a sort, believed on him, but they had not then the faith that overcometh the world. The faith I want is a sure trust and confidence in God, that, through the merits of Christ, my sins are forgiven, and I reconciled to the favour of God. I want that faith which St Paul recommends to all the world... which none can have without knowing that he hath it (though many imagine they have it, who have it not); for whosoever hath it is freed from sin, ... he is freed from fear, having peace with God through Christ. ... And he is freed from doubt. ... The Spirit itself beareth witness with his spirit, that he is a child of God.

JOURNAL, 29th JANUARY 1738

30

I have thrown up my friends, reputation, ease, country; I have put my life in my hand, wandering into strange lands; I have given my body to be devoured by the deep, parched up with heat, consumed by toil and weariness, or whatsoever God should please to bring upon me. But does all this (be it more or less, it matters not) make me acceptable to God? Does all I ever did or can know, say, give, do or suffer, justify me in his sight? Yea, or the constant use of all the means of grace?—(which nevertheless is meet, right and our bounden duty). Or that I know nothing of myself; that I am as touching outward moral righteousness blameless? Or, to come closer yet, the having a rational conviction of all the truths of Christianity? Does all this give me a claim to the holy, heavenly, divine character of a Christian? By no means.

JOURNAL, 29th JANUARY 1738

31

Go steadily and quietly on in the way wherein Providence leads you, and in every temptation he by his Spirit will clear a way for you to escape.

TO SARAH MALLETT, 1788

Proceed with much prayer, and your way will be made plain.

TO ELLEN GRETTON, 1782

Pray as you can, though you are ever so cold or dead.

TO MARY YEOMAN, 1769

FEBRUARY

1

The speaking to a congregation in the name of Christ is a thing of no small importance. You are therefore in the right, before you undertake it, to consider the matter well.

TO HENRY ANDERSON, 1791

It is certain you cannot preach the truth without offending those who preach the contrary. . . . You cannot constrain any one to go to Church; you can only advise them to do it, and encourage them by your example.

TO WALTER GRIFFITH, 1788

The plainer you speak, the more good you will do.

TO JOHN CRICKET, 1783

Wherever a man's life confirms his doctrine, God will confirm the word of his messenger.

TO ARTHUR KEENE 1784

2

Some years since, one of our preachers said: 'Mr W. has hindered me from marrying *once*, but I am resolved he shall not hinder me again.' He was as good as his word. Without asking my advice he married a woman of a thousand, who exercised him well while he lived and sent him to paradise before his time.

TO ANN BOLTON, 1780

I commend you for being exceeding wary with respect to marriage.

TO ZACHARIAH YEWDALL, 1781 and 1785

If A. Mather had not been *married*, he might have done anything.

TO SAMUEL BRADBURN, 1781

3

It is expedient that the Methodists in every part of the globe should be united together as closely as possible.

TO THOS MORRELL, 1790

Let the preachers stand firm together, and then the people will be regular; but if any of you take their part against the preacher, all will be confusion.

TO SAMUEL BARDSLEY, 1789

Unity and holiness are the two things I want among the Methodists.

TO THE REV. JOHN FLETCHER, 1766

4

Pray, whether you can or not; when you are cheerful, when you are heavy, pray—with many or few words, or none at all. You will surely find an answer of peace.

TO J. VALTON, 1764

'I love one,' said a holy man, 'that perseveres in a dry duty.'
Beware of thinking even this is labour lost. God does much work
in the heart even at those seasons.

TO MISS MARCH, 1771

One great office of prayer is to increase our desire of the things
we ask for.

NOTES ON NEW TESTAMENT, MATTHEW 6^8

5

Carefully shun every temptation, and all opportunities of sin;
especially shun as a rock the company of any person apt to tempt
or to be tempted, and consider, that the coldest water will be hot
if it be set near the fire.

THE DUTIES OF HUSBANDS AND WIVES

If you find anything hurts you or draws your soul from God, I
conjure you flee for your life! In that case, you must not stand
upon ceremony; you must escape without delay.

TO LADY MAXWELL, 1767

Prepare your soul for temptations. For how shall we conquer if
we do not fight? Go on, then, as a good soldier of Jesus Christ.

TO JOHN OGILVIE, 1786

6

Many years ago, when I was at Oxford, in a cold winter's day, a
young maid (one of those we kept at school) called upon me. I
said: 'You seem halfstarved. Have you nothing to cover you but
that thin linen gown?' She said: 'Sir, this is all I have!' I put my
hand in my pocket, but found I had scarce any money left,

having just paid away what I had. It immediately struck me: 'Will thy Master say, "Well done, good and faithful steward? Thou hast adorned thy walls with the money which might have screened this poor creature from the cold!"'

ADVICE WITH REGARD TO DRESS

7

About eight in the morning, we first set foot on American ground. It was a small uninhabited island, over against Tybee. Mr Oglethorpe led us to a rising ground, where we all kneeled down to give thanks. He then took boat for Savannah. When the rest of the people were come on shore, we called our little flock together to prayers. Several parts of the second lesson (Mark 6) were wonderfully suited to the occasion; in particular, the account of the courage and sufferings of John the Baptist; our Lord's directions to the first preachers of his Gospel, and their toiling at sea, and deliverance; with these comfortable words: 'It is I, be not afraid.'

JOURNAL, 6th FEBRUARY 1736

8

Now, this it is certain a man may want—a true trust and confidence of the mercy of God through our Lord Jesus Christ— although he can truly say: 'I am chaste; I am sober; I am just in my dealings; I help my neighbour, and use the ordinances of God.' And, however such a man may have behaved in these respects, he is not to think well of his own state till he experiences something within himself which he has not yet experienced, but which he may be beforehand assured he shall if the promises of God are true. That *something* is a living faith, 'sure trust and confidence in God that, by the merits of Christ, his sins are forgiven and he reconciled to the favour of God'. And from this will spring many other things, which till then he experienced not, as, the love of God shed abroad in his heart, the peace of God which passeth all understanding, and joy in the Holy Ghost.

TO DR STEBBING, 1739

9

I cannot deny that every follower of Christ is in his proportion the light of the world; that whosoever is such can no more be concealed than the sun in the midst of heaven; that, being set as a light in a dark place, his shining out must be the more conspicuous; that to this very end was his light given, that it might shine at least to all that look towards him; and, indeed, that there is one only way of hiding it, which is to put it out. Neither can I deny that it is the indispensable duty of every Christian to impart both light and heat to all who are willing to receive it. I am obliged likewise, unless I lie against the truth, to grant that there is not so contemptible an animal upon earth as one that drones away life, without ever labouring to promote the glory of God and the good of men.

TO HIS FATHER, 1734

10

I have often replied: (1) It were better for me to die than not to preach the gospel of Christ; yea, and in the fields, either where I may not preach in the Church or where the Church will not contain the congregation. (2) That I use the Service of the Church every Lord's Day, and it has never yet appeared to me that any rule of the Church forbids my using extempory prayer on other occasions.

But methinks I would go deeper. I would enquire, What is the end of all ecclesiastical order? Is it not to bring souls from the power of Satan to God, and to build them up in his fear and love? Order, then, is so far valuable as it answers these ends; and if it answers them not, it is nothing worth.

TO JOHN SMITH, 1746

11

I am one who for twenty years used outward works, not only 'as acts of goodness', but as commutations (though I did not indeed profess this), instead of inward holiness. I knew I was not holy. But I quieted my conscience by doing such-and-such outward works; and therefore I hoped I should go to heaven, even without inward holiness. . . .

Abundance of people I have likewise known, and many I do know at this day, who 'are so grossly superstitious as to think devotion may be put upon God instead of honesty'; as to fancy, going to Church and Sacrament will bring them to heaven, though they practise neither justice nor mercy. These are the men who make Christianity vile, who, above all others, contribute to the growth of infidelity.

TO JOHN SMITH, 1745

12

I think it great pity that the few clergymen in England who preach the three grand Scriptural doctrines—Original Sin, Justification by Faith, and Holiness consequent thereon—should have any jealousies or misunderstandings between them. What advantage must this give to the common enemy! What an hindrance is it to the great work wherein they are all engaged! How desirable is it that there should be the most open, avowed intercourse between them! . . .

For many years I have been labouring after this—labouring to unite, not scatter, the messengers of God.

TO THE REV. GEORGE DOWNING, 1761

13

Beware of bribery.

.   .   .   .   .

Have nothing to do with stolen goods. Neither sell nor buy anything that has not paid the duty—no, not if you could have it at half-price. Defraud not the King any more than your fellow subject. Never think of being religious unless you are honest. What has a thief to do with religion? ... Whatever others do, keep yourselves pure.

.   .   .   .   .

Lose no opportunity of receiving the Sacrament. All who have neglected this have suffered loss; most of them are as dead as stones; therefore be you constant therein, not only for example, but for the sake of your souls.

TO THE SOCIETIES AT BRISTOL, 1764

14

Do not encourage young raw men to exhort among you. It does little good either to you or them. Rather in every Society, where you have not an experienced preacher, let one of the leaders read the *Notes upon the New Testament* or the *Christian Library*. By this the wisest among you may profit much, a thousand times more than by listening to forward youths who neither speak English nor common sense.

.   .   .   .   .

Whoever misses his class thrice together thereby excludes himself, and the preacher that comes next ought to put out his name. ... Meet the brethren or leave them. It is not honest to profess yourself of a Society and not observe the rules of it.

TO THE SOCIETIES AT BRISTOL, 1764

15

One charge remains, which you repeat over and over, and lay a peculiar stress upon. It is the poor old worn-out tale of getting money by preaching'.... But blessed be God, my conscience is clear. My heart does not condemn me in this matter. I know, and God knoweth, that I have no desire to load myself with thick clay; that I love money no more than I love the mire in the streets; that I seek it not. And I have it not, any more than suffices for food and raiment, for the plain conveniences of life. I pay no court to it at all or to those that have it, either with cunning or without. For myself, for my own use, I raise no contributions, either great or small.

TO JOHN DOWNES, 1759

16

The weelky contributions of our community (which are freely given, not *squeezed* out of any) as well as the gifts and offerings at the Lord's Table never come into my hands. I have no concern with them, not so much as the beholding them with my eyes. They are received every week by the stewards of the Society, men of well-known character in the world; and by them constantly distributed within the week to those whom they know to be in real necessity. As to the 'very large oblations wherewith I am favoured by persons of better figure and fortune', I know nothing of them. Be so kind as to refresh my memory by mentioning a few of their names. I have the happiness of knowing some of great figure and fortune.... But if I were to say that all of them together had given me seven pounds in seven years I should say more than I could make good. And yet I doubt not but they would freely give me anything I wanted.

TO JOHN DOWNES, 1759

17

It gives me pleasure indeed to hear that God has given you resolution to join the Society. Undoubtedly you will suffer reproach on this account; but it is the reproach of Christ. And you will have large amends when the Spirit of glory and of God shall rest upon you. Yet I foresee a danger: at first you will be inclined to think that all the members of the Society are in earnest. And when you find that some are otherwise (which will always be the case in so large a body of people), then prejudice may easily steal in and exceedingly weaken your soul. O beware of this rock of offence! When you see anything amiss, remember our Lord's word: What is that to thee? Follow thou me.' And I entreat you do not regard the half-Methodists—if we must use the name. Do not mind them who endeavour to hold Christ in one hand and the world in the other.

TO LADY MAXWELL, 1764

18

Why are thousands of people starving, perishing for want, in every part of England? The fact I know; I have seen it with my eyes in every corner of the land. I have known those who could only afford to eat a little coarse food every other day. I have known one picking up stinking sprats from a dunghill and carrying them home for herself and her children.

I have known another gathering the bones which the dogs had left in the streets and making broth of them to prolong a wretched life. Such is the case at this day of multitudes of people in a land flowing, as it were, with milk and honey, abounding with all the necessities, the conveniences, the superfluities of life!

TO LLOYD'S EVENING POST, 1772

19

Why is it that not only provisions and land but well-nigh everything else is so dear? Because of the enormous taxes which are laid on almost everything that can be named. Not only abundant taxes are raised from earth and fire and water, but in England the ingenious statesmen have found a way to tax the very light! Only one element remains, and surely some man of honour will ere long contrive to tax this also. For how long shall the saucy air blow in the face of a gentleman, nay a lord, without paying for it?

But why are the taxes so high? Because of the national debt. They must be while this continues.

TO LLOYD'S EVENING POST, 1772

20

My not waiting upon you at the Town Hall was not owing to any want of respect. I reverence you for your office' sake, and much more for your zeal in the execution of it. I would to God every magistrate in the land would copy after such an example! Much less was it owing to any disaffection to His Majesty King George. But I knew not how far it might be either necessary or proper for me to appear on such an occasion. I have no fortune at Newcastle: I have only the bread I eat, and the use of a little room for a few weeks in the year.

All I can do for His Majesty, whom I honour and love (I think not less than I did my own father) is this: I cry unto God day by day, in public and in private, to put all his enemies to confusion; and I exhort all that hear me to do the same, and in their several stations to exert themselves as loyal subjects, who, so long as they fear God, cannot but honour the King.

TO THE MAYOR OF NEWCASTLE-UPON-TYNE, 1745

21

My soul has been pained day by day, even in walking the streets of Newcastle, at the senseless, shameless wickedness, the ignorant profaneness, of the poor men to whom our lives are entrusted.[1] The continual cursing and swearing, the wanton blasphemy of the soldiers in general, must needs be a torture to the sober ear, whether of a Christian or an honest infidel. Can any that either fear God or love their neighbour hear this without concern? especially if they consider the interest of our country, as well as of these unhappy men themselves. For can it be expected that God should be on their side who are daily affronting him to his face? And if God be not on their side, how little will either their number or courage or strength avail!

TO THE MAYOR OF NEWCASTLE-UPON-TYNE, 1745

22

Is there no man that careth for these souls? Doubtless there are some who ought to do so. But many of these, if I am rightly informed, receive large pay and do just nothing.

I would to God it were in my power in any degree to supply their lack of service. I am ready to do what in me lies to call these poor sinners to repentance, once or twice a day (while I remain in these parts), at any hour or at any place. And I desire no pay at all for doing this, unless what my Lord shall give me at his appearing. . . .

If it were objected that I should only fill their heads with peculiar whims and notions, that might easily be known. Only let the officers hear with their own ears; and they may judge whether I do not preach the plain principles of manly, rational religion.

TO THE MAYOR OF NEWCASTLE-UPON-TYNE, 1745

[1]15,000 troops were encamped on Newcastle Moor.

23

If it be objected: 'This conscience will make cowards of us all,' I answer: Let us judge by matter of fact. Let either friends or enemies speak. Did those who feared God behave as cowards at Fontenoy? Did John Haime, the dragoon, betray any cowardice before or after his horse sunk under him? Or did William Clements when he received the first ball in his left and the second in his right arm? Or John Evans, when the cannon-ball took off both his legs? Did he not call all about him, as long as he could speak, to praise and fear God and honour the King? as one who feared nothing but lest his last breath should be spent in vain.

.   .   .   .   .

Having myself no knowledge of the General, I took the liberty to make this offer to you. I have no interest herein; but I should rejoice to serve as I am able my King and country. If it be judged that this will be of no real service, let the proposal die and be forgotten.

TO THE MAYOR OF NEWCASTLE-UPON-TYNE, 1745

24

I have frequently observed that there are two very different ranks of Christians, both of whom may be in the favour of God—a higher and a lower rank. The latter avoid all known sin, do much good, use all the means of grace, but have little of the life of God in their souls and are much conformed to the world. The former make the Bible their whole rule, and their sole aim is the will and image of God. This they steadily and uniformly pursue, through honour and dishonour, denying themselves, and taking up their cross daily; considering one point only—how may I attain most of the mind that was in Christ, and how may I please him most?

TO THE EARL OF DARTMOUTH(?), 1770

25

You need not be reminded that there is no rank in life which exempts us from disappointment and sorrow in some kind or degree; but I must remind you there is but one belief which can support us under it.

Neither hypocrisy nor bigotry, neither the subtle arguments of infidels nor the shameful lives of Christians have yet been able to overturn the truths of revealed religion.

They contain all that is cheering—all that is consoling to the mind of man—that is congenial to the heart and adapted to his nature.

You admit their importance; you reverence their mysteries; *cherish their influences.*

TO DR WRANGEL, 1770

26

I have often thought of you as possessing everything which the world calls enviable or delightful: health, friends, leisure....Permit me to entreat you to look beyond all these for happiness.

The dangers of prosperity are great; and you seem aware of them. If poverty contracts and depresses the mind, riches sap its fortitude, destroy its vigour, and nourish its caprices.

But the chief disadvantage of an elevated situation is this: it removes us from scenes of misery and indigence; we are apt to charge the great with want of feeling, but it is rather want of consideration.

TO DR WRANGEL, 177O

27

'Child,' said my father to me when I was young, 'you think to carry everything by dint of argument. But you will find by-and-

by how very litile is ever done in the world by clear reason.' Very
little indeed! . . . Passion and prejudice govern the world, only
under the name of reason. It is our part, by religion and reason
joined, to counteract them all we can.

TO JOSEPH BENSON, 1770

28

Some time ago, since you went hence, I heard a circumstance
which gave me a good deal of concern—namely, that the College
or Academy in Georgia had swallowed up the Orphan House.
Shall I give my judgment without being asked? Methinks friendship requires that I should. Are there not, then, two points which
come in view—a point of mercy and a point of justice? With
regard to the former, may it not be inquired; Can anything on
earth be a greater charity than to bring up orphans? What is a
college or an academy compared to this? . . . I know the value of
learning, and am more in danger of prizing it too much than too
little. But still, I cannot place the giving it to five hundred
students, on a level with saving the bodies, if not the souls too,
of five hundred orphans.

TO GEORGE WHITEFIELD, 1770

29

The longer I am absent from London, and the more I attend the
Service of the Church in other places, the more I am convinced
of the unspeakable advantage which the people called Methodists
enjoy: I mean with regard to public worship. The Church where
they assemble is not gay or splendid, which might be a hindrance
on the one hand; nor sordid or dirty, which might give distaste on
the other; but plain as well as clean. The persons who assemble
there are not a gay, giddy crowd, who come chiefly to see and be
seen; nor a company of goodly, formal outside Christians, whose

religion lies in a dull round of duties; but a people most of whom do, and the rest earnestly seek to, worship God in spirit and in truth.

TO A FRIEND, 1757

MARCH

1

I can truly say I neither fear nor desire anything from your Lordship; to speak a rough truth, I do not desire any intercourse with any persons of quality in England. I mean, for my own sake; they do me no good, and I fear I can do none to them. . . .

Were I not afraid of giving your Lordship pain, I would speak yet still further. Methinks you desire I should; that is, to tell you, once for all, every thought that rises in my heart. I will then. At present I do not want *you,* but I really think you want *me.* For have you a person in all England who speaks to your Lordship so plain and downright as I do? Who remembers not the peer but the man, not the earl but the immortal spirit?

TO THE EARL OF DARTMOUTH, 1764

2

In every congregation in England which I remember to have observed there was undeniably a faulty respect of persons. In our Chapel[1] there is a place kept for Lady Huntingdon till the Creed; if she does not come before then, any one takes it that is next, as also when she is out of town. I doubt whether this respect to her be not too great; but I yield in this point to my brother's judgment.

[1]West Street Chapel.

We have no 5s. or 2s 6d. places at the Foundery, nor ever had, nor ever will. If any one asks me for a place in the gallery (we make no distinction but between men and women), he has it; I refuse none. And some hundreds have places there who pay nothing at all. First come also is first served, at every time of preaching. And the poorest have frequently the best places, because they come first.

TO MRS HUTTON, 1744

3

I have heard my mother say: 'I have frequently been as fully assured that my father's spirit was with me as if I had seen him with my eyes.' But she did not explain herself any farther. I have myself many times found on a sudden so lively an apprehension of a deceased friend that I have sometimes turned about to look; at the same time I have felt an uncommon affection for them. But I have never had anything of this kind with regard to any but those that died in faith. In dreams I have had exceeding lively conversations with them; and I doubt not but they were then very near.

TO LADY MAXWELL, 1769

4

I found my brother at Oxford, recovering from his pleurisy; and with him Peter Böhler; by whom, in the hand of the great God, I was on *Sunday*, the 5th clearly convinced of unbelief, of the want of that faith whereby alone we are saved.

Immediately it struck into my mind, 'Leave off preaching. How can you preach to others, who have not faith yourself?' I asked Böhler whether he thought I should leave it off or not. He answered: 'By no means.' I asked, 'But what can I preach?' He said: 'Preach faith till you have it; and then, because you have it, you will preach faith.'

Accordingly, *Monday*, 6, I began preaching this new doctrine, though my soul started back from the work. The first person to whom I offered salvation by faith alone, was a prisoner under sentence of death.

JOURNAL, 4th MARCH 1738

5

Ever since I heard of it first, I felt a perfect detestation of the horrid slave trade. . . . Therefore I cannot but do everything in my power to forward the glorious design of your Society.

TO GRANVILLE SHARP, 1787

'Mr Wesley informed the Committee of the great satisfaction which he had experienced when he heard of their formation. He conceived that their design, while it would destroy the slave trade, would also strike at the root of the shocking abomination of slavery. He desired to forewarn them that they must expect great difficulties and great opposition from those who were interested in the system, that they were a powerful body. . . . As to himself, he would do all he could to promote the object of their institution.'

TO THOMAS CLARKSON, 1787

6

If you go abroad, I would by no means advise you to go to France. That is no place to save expense; but it is the only place to make your sons coxcombs and your daughters coquettes. I cannot but think there is no country in Europe which would answer your design so well as Holland; and no place in Holland so well as Utrecht. It is within a day's journey of Helvoetsluys, whence you go directly by the packet for England. It is a healthful and a pleasant city, and less expensive than almost any city in France. You may have more or less company as you please. There are schools for your children; and if you should choose it, a university for your sons; and I could recommend you to some valuable acquaintance.

TO ROBERT JONES, 1784

7

I built the first preaching-house which was built for the people called Methodists—namely, at Bristol in the year 1739. And, knowing no better, I suffered the first deed of trust to be drawn in the Presbyterian form. But Mr Whitefield, hearing of this, wrote me a warm letter asking: 'Do you consider what you do? If you let the trustees name the preachers, they may exclude you and all your brethren from preaching in the houses you have built. Pray let the deed be immediately cancelled;' to which the trustees immediately agreed.

Afterwards I built the preaching-houses in Kingswood and at Newcastle-upon-Tyne. But I took care that none but myself should have any right to name preachers for them.

TO JOSEPH BENSON, 1782

8

Above thirty years ago a motion was made in Parliament for raising and embodying the militia, and for exercising them (to save time) on Sunday. When the motion was like to pass, an old gentleman stood up and said: 'Mr Speaker, I have one objection to this: I believe an old book called the Bible.' The members looked at one another, and the motion was dropped.

Must not all others who believe the Bible have the very same objection? And from what I have seen, I cannot but think these are still three-fourths of the nation.... Would not all England, would not all Europe, consider this as a virtual repeal of the Bible? And would not all serious persons say: 'We have little religion in the land now; but by this step we shall have less still.'

TO THE EARL OF SHELBURNE, 1782

9

Be active, be diligent; avoid all laziness, sloth, indolence. Fly from every degree, every appearance of it; else you will never be more than half a Christian.

Be cleanly. In this let the Methodists take pattern by the Quakers. Avoid all nastiness, dirt, slovenliness, both in your person, clothes, house, and all about you. Do not stink above ground. This is a bad fruit of laziness; use all diligence to be clean.

Whatever clothes you have, let them be whole; no rents, no tatters, no rags. These are a scandal to either man or woman, being another fruit of vile laziness. Mend your clothes, or I shall never expect you to mend your lives. Let none ever see a ragged Methodist.

TO RICHARD STEELE, 1769

10

Be merciful after your power; give as God enables you. If you are not in pressing want, give something, and you will be no poorer for it. Grudge not, fear not; lend unto the Lord, and he will surely repay. If you earn but three shillings a week and give a penny out of it, you will never want. But I do not say this to you who have ten or fifteen shillings a week and give only a penny! To see this has often grieved my spirit. I have been ashamed for you, if you have not been ashamed for yourself.

Why, by the same rule that you give a penny, that poor man should give a peppercorn!...Give in proportion to your substance. You can better afford a shilling than he a penny.

TO THE SOCIETIES AT BRISTOL, 1764

11

I really hope the Sunday Schools will be productive of great good to the nation. They spread wider and wider, and are likely to reach every part of the kingdom.

TO THE REV. JOHN FLETCHER, 1785

Our Sunday Schools at Bolton contain upward of eight hundred children, and are all taught by our own brethren *without pay*.

TO ALEXANDER SUTER, 1787

The Sunday Schools have been of great use in every part of England, and to assist in any of them is a noble employment.

TO HIS NIECE, SARAH WESLEY, 1788

Take care of the rising generation.

TO THOMAS RANKIN, 1767

12

You are to cure Robert Swan of preaching too long.

TO CHRISTOPHER HOPPER, 1773

If any other of the preachers exceed their time (about an hour in the whole Service), I hope you will always put them in mind what is the Methodist rule. People imagine the longer the sermon is the more good it will do. This is a grand mistake. The help done on earth God doth it himself; and he doth not need that we should use many words.

TO MRS JOHNSTON, 1777

13

It is a constant rule with us that no preacher should preach above twice a day, unless on Sunday or on some extraordinary time; and then he may preach three times. We know nature cannot long bear the preaching oftener than this, and therefore to do it is a degree of self-murder. Those of our preachers who would not follow this advice have all repented when it was too late.

I likewise advise all our preachers not to preach above an hour at a time, prayer and all; and not to speak louder either in preaching or prayer than the number of hearers requires.

TO THOMAS CAPITER, 1753

14

Sometimes I cannot do good to others because I am unwilling to do it: shame or pain is in the way; and I do not desire to serve God at so dear a rate. Sometimes I cannot do the good I desire to do because I am in other respects too unholy. I know within myself, were I fit to be so employed, God would employ me in this work. But my heart is too unclean. . . . Sometimes I cannot accomplish the good I am employed in, because I do not pray more, and more fervently; and sometimes, even when I do pray, and that instantly, because I am not worthy that my prayer should be heard. Sometimes I dare not attempt to assist my neighbour, because I know the narrowness of my heart, that it cannot attend to many things without utter confusion and dissipation of thought.

TO HIS FATHER, 1734

15

As many persons desire to know where I am from this time till the Conference, I here set down my route, which, if God permit, I shall keep till that time.

March

Monday, 15, Stroud; 16, Gloucester; 17, Worcester; 18, Stourport; 19, Birmingham.

Monday, 22, Wednesbury; 23, Dudley and Wolverhampton; 24, Madeley; 25, Salop; 26, Madeley; 27, Newcastle-under-Lyme; 28, Burslem.

Monday, 29, Congleton; 30, Macclesfield.

(Between 1st and 29th April Wesley visited twenty places from Stockport to Otley. He then moved on from York to Aberdeen. He was in his eighty-seventh year.)

N.B. I have not yet finally settled the rest of my plan. . . . Many persons are continually teasing me to visit more places. Now let them judge whether I have not work enough.

TO PREACHERS AND FRIENDS, 1790

16

Are all our preachers merciful to their beasts?

Perhaps not. Every one ought, not only to ride it moderately, but also to see with his own eyes, his horse rubbed, fed and bedded.

.   .   .   .   .

What is it best to take just after preaching?

Lemonade; candied orange peel or a little soft, warm ale. But egg and wine is downright poison.

MINUTES OF CONVERSATIONS, 1744

Let none of you preachers touch any spirituous liquors upon any account.

TO FRANCIS WOLFE, 1782

17

I know, were I myself to preach one whole year in one place, I should preach both myself and most of my congregation asleep. Nor can I believe it was ever the will of our Lord that any congregation should have one teacher only. We have found by long and constant experience that a frequent change of teachers is best. This preacher has one talent, that another. No one whom I ever yet knew has all the talents which are needful for beginning, continuing and perfecting the work of grace in a whole congregation.

TO THE REV. MR WALKER, 1756

Hear what preacher you will; but hear the voice of God, and beware of prejudice and every unkind temper.

TO MISS ——, 1759

18

As Satan turned the heart of man, from the Creator to the creature; so the Son of God turns his heart back again, from the creature to the Creator.

He entrusts us with only an exceeding small share of knowledge in our present state, lest our knowledge should interfere with our humility, and we should again affect to be as gods.

Here then, we see in the clearest, strongest light, what is real religion: a restoration of man, by Christ, not only to the favour, but likewise to the image of God.

THE END OF CHRIST'S COMING

19

One cannot but observe throughout the whole story of Adam and Eve, the inexpressible tenderness and lenity of the almighty Creator from whom they had revolted: 'And the Lord God called unto Adam, and said unto him: "Where art thou?" ' Thus graciously calling him to return, who would otherwise have eternally fled from God.

.   .   .   .   .

'The woman was deceived', says the Apostle. She believed a lie; She gave more credit to the word of the devil than to the word of God. And unbelief brought forth actual sin.

.   .   .   .   .

Behold then both the justice and mercy of God! His justice in punishing sin. . . . And his mercy in providing a universal remedy for a universal evil! . . . That as in Adam all died, so in Christ all might be made alive.

THE FALL OF MAN

20

Be serious and frequent in the examination of your heart and life. . . . Every evening review your carriage through the day; what you have done or thought that was unbecoming your character; whether your heart has been instant upon religion and indifferent to the world? Have a special care of two portions of time, namely, morning and evening; the morning to forethink what you have to do, and the evening to examine whether you have done what you ought.

Let every action have reference to your whole life, and not to a part only. Let all your subordinate ends be suitable to the great end of your living. Exercise yourself unto godliness.

CONSCIENCE

21

Consult duty; not events. We have nothing to do but to mind our duty.

.   .   .   .   .

What advice you would give another, take yourself.

.   .   .   .   .

Do nothing on which you cannot pray for a blessing. Every action of a Christian that is good is sanctified by the Word and prayer. It becomes not a Christian to do anything so trivial that he cannot pray over it.

.   .   .   .   .

Above all, sooner forget your Christian name than forget Christ.

CONSCIENCE

22

But sometimes this excellent quality, tenderness of conscience, is carried to an extreme. We find some who fear where no fear is; who are continually condemning themselves without cause; imagining some things to be sinful, which the Scripture nowhere condemns; and supposing other things to be their duty, which the Scripture nowhere enjoins. This is properly termed a scrupulous conscience, and is a sore evil. It is highly expedient to yield to it as little as possible; rather it should be a matter of earnest prayer that you may be delivered from this sore evil, and may recover a sound mind.

CONSCIENCE

23

What, then, shall I say of Predestination? An everlasting purpose of God to deliver some from damnation does, I suppose, exclude all from that deliverance who are not chosen. And if it was inevitably decreed from eternity that such a determinate part of mankind should be saved, and none beside them, a vast majority of the world were only born to eternal death, without so much as a possibility of avoiding it. How is this consistent with either the Divine justice or mercy? Is it merciful to ordain a creature to everlasting misery? Is it just to punish a man for crimes which he could not but commit? How is man, if necessarily determined to one way of acting, a free agent? To lie under either a physical or a moral necessity is entirely repugnant to human liberty.

TO HIS MOTHER, 1725

24

What are all the absurd opinions of all the Romanists in the world compared to that of absolute Predestination, that the God of Love, the wise, just, merciful Father of the spirits of all flesh, has from all eternity fixed an absolute, unchangeable, irresistible decree that part of mankind shall be saved, do what they will, and the rest damned, do what they can!

THE TRINITY

I do not believe the doctrine of absolute Predestination.

REMARKS ON MR HILL'S REVIEW

25

Another of his [Thomas à Kempis'] tenets . . . is that all mirth is vain and useless, if not sinful. But why then, does the Psalmist so often exhort us to rejoice in the Lord and tell us that it becomes the just to be joyful? I think one could hardly desire a more express text than that in the 68th Psalm: 'Let the righteous rejoice and be glad in the Lord. Let them also be merry and joyful.' And he seems to carry the matter as much too far on the other side afterwards, where he asserts that nothing is an affliction to a good man, and that he ought to thank God even for sending him misery. This, in my opinion, is contrary to God's design in afflicting us.

TO HIS MOTHER, 1725

26

I can't think that when God sent us into the world, he had irreversibly decreed that we should be perpetually miserable in it. If it be so, the very endeavour after happiness in this life is a sin; as it is acting in direct contradiction to the very design of our creation. What are become of all the innocent comforts and pleasures of life, if it is the intent of our Creator that we should never taste them? If our taking up the cross implies our bidding adieu to all joy and satisfaction, how it is reconcilable with what Solomon so expressly affirms of religion—that her ways are ways of pleasantness and all her paths are peace?

TO HIS MOTHER, 1725

27

I am no politician; politics lie quite outside my province. . . .
Perhaps you will say: 'Nay, every Englishman is a politician. . . . We can in a trice reform the State, point out every blunder of this or that Minister, and tell every step they ought to take to be arbiters of all Europe.'
I grant every cobbler, tinker, porter and hackneycoachman can do this. But I am not so deep learned; while they are sure of

everything, I am in a manner sure of nothing, except of that very little which I see with my own eyes or hear with my own ears. However, since you desire me to tell you what I think, I will do it with all openness. Only please to remember I do not take upon me to dictate either to you or to any one.

TO A FRIEND, 1768

28

As long as we dwell in a house of clay it is liable to affect the mind; sometimes by dulling or darkening the understanding, and sometimes more directly by damping and depressing the soul and sinking it into distress and heaviness. In this state doubt or fear of one kind or another will naturally arise. And the prince of this world, who well knows whereof we are made, will not fail to improve the occasion, in order to disturb, though he cannot pollute, the heart which God hath cleansed from all unrighteousness.

TO MISS MARCH, 1771

29

If one wheel in a machine gets out of its place, what disorder must ensue! In the Methodist discipline the wheels regularly stand thus: the assistant,[1] the preachers, the stewards, the leaders, the people.

But here the leaders, who are the lowest wheel but one, were got quite out of their place. They were got at the top of all, above the stewards, the preachers, and above the assistant himself.

To this chiefly I impute the gradual decay of the work of God in Dublin. . . . But it may be effectually remedied now. . . . For the time to come, let each wheel keep its own place. Let the assistant, the preachers, the stewards, the leaders, know and

[1]The Superintendent.

execute their several offices. Let none encroach upon another.

JOURNAL, 3rd APRIL 1771

30

If by Catholic principles you mean any other than scriptural, they weigh nothing with me. I allow no other rule, whether of faith or practice, than the Holy Scriptures; but on scriptural principles I do not think it hard to justify whatever I do. God in Scripture commands me, according to my power, to instruct the ignorant, reform the wicked, confirm the virtuous. Man forbids me to do this in another's parish; that is, in effect, to do it at all, seeing I have now no parish of my own, nor probably ever shall. Whom, then, shall I hear, God or man? . . .

Suffer me now to tell you my principles in this matter. I look upon all the world as my parish; thus far I mean, that in whatever part of it I am I judge it meet, right and my bounden duty to declare unto all that are willing to hear, the glad tidings of salvation.

TO THE REV. JAMES HERVEY, 1739

31

You abound in leisure; I abound in work.

TO WM GREEN, 1789

Every good purpose will cool and die away if it is not as soon as possible put in execution. Only let us not undertake too much at a time.

TO PEARD DICKINSON, 1789

You must not give place—no, not for a day—to inactivity.
Nothing is more apt to grow upon the soul; the less you speak or
act for God, the less you may.

TO ELIZABETH RITCHIE 1774

Who would wish to live for any meaner purpose than to serve
God in our generation?

TO R. C. BRACKENBURY, 1783

APRIL

1

Thus it was that two young men without a name, without friends, without either power or fortune, set out from College with principles totally different from those of the common people, to oppose all the world, learned and unlearned, to combat popular prejudices of every kind. Our first principle directly attacked all the wickedness, our second all the bigotry, in the world. Thus they attempted a reformation, not of opinions (feathers, trifles not worth the naming), but of men's tempers and lives; of vice in every kind; of everything contrary to justice, mercy or truth. And for this it was that they carried their lives in their hands, that both the great vulgar and the small looked upon them as mad dogs and treated them as such.

TO SAMUEL SPARROW, 1773

2

A few days since, Mr Whitefield and I desired a friend to ask your advice, to whom it would be proper to make an offer of raising a company of volunteers for His Majesty's service. We apprehended the number would be about five hundred. Finding Mr Whitefield has since been persuaded that such an offer is premature, I am constrained to make the following independently of him:

To raise for His Majesty's service at least two hundred volunteers, to be supported by contributions among themselves; and to be ready in case of an invasion to act for a year (if needed so long) at His Majesty's pleasure. . . .

If this be acceptable to His Majesty, they beg to have arms out of the Tower, giving the usual security for their return, and some of His Majesty's sergeants to instruct them in the military exercise.

TO THE HON. JAMES WEST, M.P., 1756

3

You think the mode of baptism is necessary to salvation. I deny that even baptism itself is so; if it were, every Quaker must be damned, which I can in no wise believe. I hold nothing to be (strictly speaking) necessary to salvation but the mind which was in Christ . . . I wish your zeal was better employed than in persuading men to be either dipped or sprinkled. . . .

I cannot answer it to God to spend any part of that precious time, every hour of which I can employ in what directly tends to the promoting of his love among men, in oppugning or defending this or that form of Church government. . . . I am called to other work; not to make Church of England men or Baptists, but Christians, men of faith and love.

TO GILBERT BOYCE (BAPTIST MINISTER), 1750

4

About four in the afternoon I set out for Frederica, in a *pettiawga*—a sort of flat-bottomed barge. The next evening we anchored near Skidoway Island, where the water, at flood, was twelve or fourteen foot deep. I wrapped myself up from head to foot, in a large cloak, to keep off the sand flies, and lay down on the quarter deck. Between one and two I waked under water, being so fast asleep that I did not find where I was till my mouth was full of it. Having left my cloak, I know not how, upon deck, I swam round to the other side of the *pettiawga,* where a boat was tied, and climbed up by the rope without any hurt, more than wetting my clothes.

JOURNAL, 4th APRIL 1736

5

Since I was six years old, I never met with such a severe trial as for some days past. For ten years God has been preparing a fellow labourer for me by a wonderful train of providences. Last year I was convinced of it; therefore I delayed not, but, as I thought, made all sure beyond a danger of disappointment. But we were soon afterwards torn asunder by a whirlwind. In a few months the storm was over. . . . But it soon returned . . . I fasted and prayed and strove all I could; but the sons of Zeruiah were too strong for me. The whole world fought against me. Then was the word fulfilled: 'Son of man, behold! I take from thee the desire of thine eyes at a stroke; yet thou shalt not lament, neither shall thy tears run down.'

TO THOMAS BIGG, 1749

6

It is hard to find words in the language of men to explain the deep things of God. Indeed, there are none that will adequately express what the children of God experience. But perhaps one might say the testimony of the Spirit is an inward impression on the soul, whereby the Spirit of God directly witnesses to my spirit, that I am a child of God; that Jesus Christ hath loved me and given himself for me; and that all my sins are blotted out, and I, even I, am reconciled to God.

THE WITNESS OF THE SPIRIT (I)

7

Meantime let it be observed, I do not mean hereby, that the Spirit of God testifies this by an outward voice; no, nor always by an inward voice, although he may do this sometimes. Neither do I suppose that he always applies to the heart (though he often may) one or more texts of Scripture. But he so works upon the soul by his immediate influence, and by a strong though inexplicable operation, that the stormy wind and troubled waves subside, and there is a sweet calm; the heart resting is in the arms of Jesus, and the sinner being clearly satisfied that God is reconciled, that all his iniquities are forgiven, and his sins covered.

THE WITNESS OF THE SPIRIT (II)

8

Now, in order to this, there is absolutely required, first, a right understanding of the Word of God, of his holy and acceptable and perfect Will concerning us, as it is revealed therein. For it is impossible we should walk by a rule, if we do not know what it means. There is, secondly, required (which how few have attained!) a true knowledge of ourselves, of our inward tempers and outward conversation, seeing, if we know them not, it is not possible that we should compare them with our rule. There is required, thirdly, an agreement of our hearts and lives with that rule. For without this, if we have any conscience at all, it can only be an evil conscience. There is, fourthly, required, an inward perception of this agreement with our rule: and this habitual perception, this inward consciousness itself, is properly a *good conscience*.

THE WITNESS OF THE SPIRT (III)

9

God has made us thinking beings, capable of perceiving what is present, and of reflecting or looking back on what is past. In particular, we are capable of perceiving whatsoever passes in our own hearts or lives; of knowing whatsoever we feel or do; and that either while it passes or when it is past. This we mean when we say, man is a *conscious* being; he hath a consciousness or inward perception, both of things present and past, relating to himself, of his own tempers and outward behaviour. But what we really term *conscience* implies somewhat more than this. It is not barely the knowledge of our present or the remembrance of our preceding life ... its main business is to excuse or accuse, to approve or disapprove, to acquit or condemn. We may understand by conscience, a faculty or power, implanted by God, in every soul that comes into the world, of perceivng what is right or wrong in his own heart or life.

THE WITNESS OF THE SPIRIT (III)

10

But what is the rule whereby men are to judge of right and wrong? Whereby their conscience is to be directed? ... The Christian rule of right and wrong is the Word of God, the writings of the Old and New Testament. ... This is a lantern unto the Christian's feet, and a light in all his paths. This alone he receives as his rule of right or wrong, of whatever is really good or evil. He esteems nothing good but what is here enjoined, either directly or by plain consequence; he accounts nothing evil but what is here forbidden, either in terms or by undeniable inference.

THE WITNESS OF THE SPIRIT (III)

11

Why is there sin in the world? Because man was created in the image of God, because he is not mere matter—a clod of earth, a lump of clay—without sense or understanding, but a spirit like his Creator, a being endued not only with sense and understanding, but also with a will exerting itself in various affections. To crown all the rest he was endued with liberty: a power of directing his own affections and actions, a capacity of determining himself or of choosing good or evil. Indeed, had not man been endued with this, all the rest would have been of no use. Had he not been a free as well as an intelligent being, his understanding would have been as incapable of holiness or any kind of virtue as a tree or a block of marble. And, having this power, a power of choosing good or evil, he chose evil..

THE FALL OF MAN

12

Do just the same in the absence of your employer as you do when under his eye. Let his absence or presence make no difference to your industry and activity.

Equally dishonest it is to hurt or waste anything, or to let it be lost through your carelessness or negligence.

Whatever is committed to your trust, whether within doors or without, so carefully preserve that it be not lost, spoiled or impaired under your hands. If you see any damage done to your employer's goods, redress it yourself, if you can; if you cannot, immediately make it known to your employer, that he may find means of redressing it. And not only preserve, but do all that in you lies to increase your employer's goods.

DIRECTIONS TO SERVANTS

13

Never, on any account, give a child anything that it cries for. For it is a true observation (and you may make the experiment as often as you please), if you give a child what it cries for, you *pay him for crying;* and then he will certainly cry again. 'But if I do not give it him when he cries, he will scream all day long.' If he does, it is your own fault; for it is in your power effectually to prevent it. For no mother need suffer a child to cry aloud after it is a year old. 'Why, it is impossible to hinder it!' So many suppose; but it is an entire mistake. . . . My own mother had ten children, each of whom had spirit enough. Yet not one of them was ever heard to cry aloud, after it was a year old.

THE EDUCATION OF CHILDREN

14

Possibly you may have another difficulty to encounter, and one of a still more trying nature. Your mother, or your husband's mother, may live with you; and you will do well to shew her all possible respect. But let her on no account have the least share in the management of your children. She would undo all that you had done; she would give them their own will in all things. . . . In fourscore years I have not met with one woman that knew how to manage grandchildren. My own mother who governed her children so well, could never govern one grandchild. In every other point obey your mother. Give up your will to hers. But with regard to the management of your children, steadily keep the reins in your own hands.

THE EDUCATION OF CHILDREN

15

The generality of parents feed and increase the natural falsehood of their children . . . Let the wise parent teach them that the author of all falsehood is the devil. . . . Teach them to abhor and despise, not only lying but all equivocating, all cunning and dissimulation. Use every means to give them a love of truth: of veracity, sincerity and simplicity, and of openness both of spirit and behaviour. . . . And from their very infancy, sow the seeds of justice in their hearts, and train them up in the exactest practice of it. If possible, teach them the love of justice, and that in the least things as well as the greatest. Impress upon their minds the old proverb: 'He that will steal a penny, will steal a pound.' Habituate them to render unto all their due, even to the uttermost farthing.

THE EDUCATION OF CHILDREN

16

You should particularly endeavour to instruct your children, early, plainly, frequently and patiently. Instruct them early from the first hour that you perceive reason begins to dawn. Truth may then begin to shine upon the mind far earlier than we are apt to suppose. And whoever watches the first opening of the understanding, may, by little and little, supply fit matter for it to work upon, and may turn the eye of the soul toward good things, as well as toward bad or trifling ones. Whenever a child begins to speak, you may be assured reason begins to work. I know no cause why a parent should not just then begin to speak of the best things, the things of God.

FAMILY RELIGION

17

What can parents do, and mothers more especially, with regard to the atheism that is natural to all the children of men? How is this fed by the generality of parents, even those that love, or, at least, fear God, while in spending hours, perhaps days with their children, they hardly name the Name of God?

Do not parents feed the atheism of their children further by ascribing the works of creation to nature? Does not the common way of talking about nature leave God quite out of the question?

From the first dawn of reason continually inculcate: God is in this and every place. God made you and me, and the earth, and the sun, and the moon, and everything. And everything is his: heaven and earth and all that is therein. God orders all things. He makes the sun shine, and the wind blow, and the trees bear fruit. Nothing comes by chance: that is a silly word; there is no such thing as chance.

THE EDUCATION OF CHILDREN

18

I distinctly remember that even in my childhood, even when I was at school, I have often said: 'They say the life of a schoolboy is the happiest in the world; but I am sure I am not happy. For I am not content, and so cannot be happy.' When I had lived a few years longer, being in the vigour of youth, a stranger to pain and sickness, and particularly to lowness of spirits (which I do not remember to have felt one quarter of an hour ever since I was born), having plenty of all things, in the midst of sensible and amiable friends, who loved me, and I loved them, and being in the way of life which, of all others, suited my inclinations, still I was not happy! I wondered why I was not, and could not imagine what the reason was. The reason certainly was: I did not know God, the source of present as well as eternal happiness.

SPIRITUAL WORSHIP

19

In the ancient Church, when baptism was administered, there were usually two or more *Sponsors* (so Tertullian calls them), for every person to be baptised. As these were *witnesses* before God and the Church, of the solemn engagement those persons entered into, so they *undertook* (as the very word implies) to watch over those souls in a peculiar manner, to instruct, admonish, exhort, and build them up in the faith once delivered to the saints. These were considered as a kind of spiritual parents to the baptised.

See the child be taught . . . the Creed, the Lord's Prayer, and the Ten Commandments, and all other things which a Christian ought to know and believe to his soul's health, and that he may be virtuously brought up to lead a godly and a Christian life. . . . Waive every other consideration, and choose for their sponsors those persons alone who truly fear and serve God.

CONCERNING GODFATHERS AND GODMOTHERS

20

A conversation I had yesterday with Brother Proctor determined me to write immediately. The person at Birr will not do; not only as she is far too young, little more than a child; but as she has only little, if any, Christian experience. You want a woman of middle age, well-tried, of good sense, and of deep experience. Such a one in every respect is Molly Penington; but whether she is willing to marry or no, I cannot tell. If she is, I hardly know her fellow in the kingdom. If I meet with any, I will send you word.

TO THOMAS MASON, 1771

21

I returned to England in the beginning of February 1738. I was now in haste to retire to Oxford and bury myself in my beloved obscurity. But I was detained in London, week after week, by the Trustees for the Colony of Georgia. In the meantime I was continually importuned to preach in one or another Church, and that not only morning, afternoon and night on Sundays, but on weekdays also. As I was lately come from a far country, vast multitudes flocked together. But in a short time, partly because of those unwieldy crowds, partly because of my unfashionable doctrine, I was excluded from one and another Church, and, at length, shut out of all. Not daring to be silent, after a short struggle between honour and conscience, I made a virtue of necessity, and preached in the middle of Moorfields.

SERMON AT THE FOUNDATION OF CITY ROAD CHAPEL

22

Here were thousands upon thousands, abundantly more than any Church could contain; and numbers among them who never went to any Church or place of worship at all. More and more of them were cut to the heart, and came to me all in tears, enquiring with the utmost eagerness what they must do to be saved. I said: 'If all of you will meet me on Thursday evening, I will advise you as well as I can.' The first evening about twelve persons came; the next week thirty or forty. When they were increased to about a hundred, I took down their names and places of abode, intending, as often as it was convenient, to call upon them at their own houses. Thus, without any previous plan or design, began the Methodist Society in England.

SERMON AT THE FOUNDATION OF CITY ROAD CHAPEL

23

This revival of religion has spread to such a degree as neither we nor our fathers had known. How *extensive* has it been! There is scarce a considerable town in the kingdom where some have not been made witnesses of it. It has spread to every age and sex, to most orders and degrees of men; and even to abundance of those who, in time past, were accounted monsters of wickedness.

Consider the *swiftness* as well as extent of it. In what age has such a number of sinners been recovered in so short a time from the error of their ways?

SERMON AT THE FOUNDATION OF CITY ROAD CHAPEL

24

We may likewise observe the *depth* of the work so extensively and swiftly wrought. Multitudes have been thoroughly convinced of sin; and, shortly after, so filled with joy and love, that whether they were in the body or out of the body, they could hardly tell. And in the power of this love, they have trampled under foot whatever the world accounts either terrible or desirable, having evidenced, in the severest trials, an invariable and tender good-will to mankind, and all the fruits of holiness. Now so deep a repentance, so strong a faith, such fervent love, and such unblemished holiness, wrought in so many persons in so short a time, the world has not seen for many ages.

SERMON AT THE FOUNDATION OF CITY ROAD CHAPEL

25

Many ask: 'Why do you say the Methodists form no distinct party? That they do not leave the Church? Are there not thousands of Methodists who have, in fact, left the Church? Who never attend the Church Service? Never receive the Lord's Supper there? Nay, who speak against the Church, even with bitterness, in public and private.'

I am glad of so public an opportunity of explaining this, in order to which, it will be necessary to look back some years. The Methodists at Oxford were all one body, and, as it were, one soul; zealous for the religion of the Bible, of the Primitive Church, and, in consequence, of the Church of England; as they believed it came nearer the Scriptural and primitive plan than any other national Church upon earth. When my brother and I returned from Georgia we were in the same sentiments. . . . Thus far, therefore, all the Methodists were firm to the Church of England.

SERMON AT THE FOUNDATION OF CITY ROAD CHAPEL

26

Brethren, I presume the greater part of you also are members of the Church of England. So at least you are called; but you are not so indeed unless you are witnesses of the religion above described. And are you really such? Judge not one another; but every man look into his own bosom. How stands the matter in your own breast? Examine your conscience before God. Are you a happy partaker of this scriptural, this truly primitive religion? Are you a lover of God and all mankind? Does your heart glow with gratitude to the Giver of every good and perfect gift? Is your soul warm with benevolence to all mankind?

SERMON AT THE FOUNDATION OF CITY ROAD CHAPEL

27

Come, and let us magnify the Lord together, and labour to promote his Kingdom upon earth. Let us join hearts and hands in this blessed work, in striving to bring glory to God in the highest, by establishing peace and goodwill among men, to the uttermost of our power. First, let our hearts be joined herein; let us unite our wishes and prayers; let our whole soul pant after a general revival of pure religion and undefiled, the restoration of the image of God, pure love, in every child of man. Then, let us endeavour to promote, in our several stations, this Scriptural, primitive religion; let us with all diligence diffuse the religion of love among all.

SERMON AT THE FOUNDATION OF CITY ROAD CHAPEL

28

Methodism, so called, is the old religion, the religion of the Bible, the religion of the Primitive Church, the religion of the Church of England. This *old religion* is no other than love, the love of God and of all mankind. . . . This love is the great medicine of life, the never-failing remedy for all the evils of a disordered world, for all the miseries and vices of men. Wherever this is, there are virtue and happiness going hand in hand.

SERMON AT THE FOUNDATION OF CITY ROAD CHAPEL

29

A string of opinions is no more Christian faith than a string of beads is Christian holiness. It is not an assent to any opinion or any number of opinions. A man may assent to three or three-and-twenty creeds, he may assent to all the Old and New Testament (at least, as far as he understands them), and yet have no Christian faith at all. The faith by which the promise is attained is represented by Christianity as a power, wrought by the Almighty in an immortal spirit inhabiting a house of clay, to see into the world of spirits. . . . To believe (in the Christian sense) is to walk in the light of eternity. . . . Does not every thinking man want a window, not so much in his neighbour's as in his own breast? He wants an opening there of whatever kind, that might let in light from eternity.

TO DR MIDDLETON, 1748-9

30

Be peculiarly careful to set before your children the copies and patterns of the virtues which you teach. And let them neither see nor hear anything from you which you would not desire to have copied by them. . . . We ought to reverence and stand in awe of children, that nothing may be spoken or done in their sight, which may taint their tender minds.

With regard to their spiritual good, your first labour of love is to present them to God in baptism. You are to inure them to good, to instruct and admonish them, to educate them in the knowledge and fear of God, to season their minds as early as possible with the fundamental truths of religion, and in such manner as is best suited to their capacity, to train them up in all holiness. Every instruction should be seconded by example.

THE DUTIES OF HUSBANDS AND WIVES

MAY

1

Sickness and weakness are things which of themselves are hard enough to be borne. There needs not the addition of unkindness to make the burden heavier.

. . . . .

You must faithfully keep each other's secrets. A man may have occasion to acquaint his wife with things he would not reveal to others; so a woman to acquaint her husband.

. . . . .

It is an infallible truth that there is no comfortable living with one whom you cannot trust.

. . . . .

If the husband puts a fool's coat upon his back, can he blame his wife for laughing at him?

THE DUTIES OF HUSBANDS AND WIVES

2

Let marriage also be sanctified or made holy by prayer. Solemnly pray for the blessing of God. . . . As therefore it is a brutish profaneness for any man to sit down to his table, as a horse to the manger, without asking the blessing of God first, and to return from it as a fox from his prey, without praising him that gave him food and appetite; so it is a great licentiousness for married persons to come together, as it were, brute beasts, without either prayer or thanksgiving..

This yields a good instruction to young unmarried people, not to rush unadvisedly into this state. A thing of so difficult a nature should not be so hastily undertaken. If they get not first their hearts full of grace, and their heads full of wisdom, they will find their hands full of work, a house full of trouble, and a life full of woe.... He that leaps over a broad ditch with a short staff, will fall into the midst; and he that enters into marriage without grace, shall fall into disquietude and vexation.

THE DUTIES OF HUSBANDS AND WIVES

3

Parents are under a peculiar obligation, by daily and earnest prayer, to commend their children to God's protection and blessing. You are, secondly, to bless them by your piety. See that you be such persons in all holy conversation, that from you the blessing of God may descend upon your posterity.

THE DUTIES OF HUSBANDS AND WIVES

The debt which a child owes to a parent is so inconceivably great, that he can never hope fully to discharge it himself. He is therefore to seek the assistance of God, and continually to beg him that has all power in heaven and earth, to return whatever good his parents have done him, sevenfold into their own bosom.

DIRECTIONS TO CHILDREN

4

Of all gossiping, religious gossiping is the worst; it adds hypocrisy to uncharitableness, and effectually does the work of the devil in the name of the Lord. The leaders in every Society may do much towards driving it out from among the Methodists. Let them in the band or class observe: (1) 'Now we are to talk of *no absent persons,* but simply of God and our own souls;' (2) 'Let the rule of our conversation here be the rule of all our conversation. Let us observe it (unless in some necessarily exempt cases) at all times and in all places.' If this be frequently inculcated, it will have an excellent effect.

TO PHILOTHEA BRIGGS, 1772

5

Keep close to your rule, the Word of God, and to your guide, the Spirit of God, and never be afraid of expecting too much.

TO MISS MARCH, 1761

We are called to propagate Bible religion through the land—that is, faith working by love, holy tempers and holy lives. Let us do it with our might.

TO JOSEPH BENSON, 1777

6

Your preaching frequently will be no hindrance, but rather a furtherance (to your health), provided you have the resolution always to observe the Methodist rule of concluding the Service within the hour.

TO R. C. BRACKENBURY, 1781

Be not at every one's call. . . . Never continue the Service above an hour at once, singing, *preaching,* prayer and all. You are not to judge by your own *feelings,* but by the word of God. Never scream. Never speak above the natural pitch of your voice; it is disgustful to the hearers. It gives them pain, not pleasure. And it is destroying yourself.

TO SARAH MALLETT, 1789

7

If you do build, take care to have windows enough and two broad doors; and do not build a scarecrow of a house.

TO JOHN BREDIN, 1789

A preaching-house can't be too light or too airy? Therefore your windows must be large. And let them be sashes, opening downward; otherwise the air coming in would give people cold. . . . and see that whatever is done be done neat and strong.

TO EDWARD BOLTON, 1769

You must not undertake any building till two-thirds of the money it will cost are subscribed.

TO ROBERT COSTERDINE, 1769

8

No preacher is to preach three times in a day to the same congregation. It is neither good for his body nor soul.

TO MR YORK, 1790

Always conclude the Service within the hour.

TO JAS RIDALL, 1787

Speak plain to Brother Ward and Foster, and tell them from me: 'Unless you can and will leave off preaching long, I shall think it my duty to prevent you preaching at all among the Methodists.'

TO JEREMIAH BRETTALL, 1781

9

Why have you not set on foot a weekly subscription in order to lessen your debt? Have neither the preachers nor the people any spirit? Who begins? I will give two shillings and sixpence a week (for a year), if all of you together will make up twenty shillings.

TO WM MEARS, 1790

Mr Churchey is an honest attorney! Therefore he is poor, and has eight children. Give me a guinea for him, for his own sake, for God's sake, and for the sake of John Wesley.

PROPOSALS FOR PRINTING BY SUBSCRIPTION
WALTER CHURCHEY'S POEMS, 1789

If the people were more alive to God, they would be more liberal. There is money enough, and particularly in Somersetshire.

TO JOHN MASON, 1784

10

All the blessings which God hath bestowed upon man are of his mere grace, bounty or favour; his free, undeserved favour; favour altogether undeserved; man having no claim to the least of his mercies. It was free grace that formed man of the dust of the ground, and breathed into him a living soul and stamped on that soul the image of God, and put all things under his feet. The same free grace continues to us, at this day, life and breath and all things, For there is nothing we are or have or do which can deserve the least thing at God's hand.

SALVATION BY FAITH

11

I am shortly to take my Master's degree. As I shall from that time be less interrupted by business not of my own choosing, I have drawn up for myself a scheme of studies, from which I do not intend, for some years at least, to vary. I am perfectly come over to your opinion that there are many truths it is not worth while to know. Curiosity, indeed, might be a sufficient plea for our laying out some time upon them, if we had half a dozen centuries of life to come; but, methinks it is great ill-husbandry to spend a considerable part of the small pittance now allowed us in what makes us neither a quick nor a sure return.

TO HIS MOTHER, 1727

12

It was in pursuance of an advice given by Bishop Taylor, in his *Rules for Holy Living and Dying,* that about fifteen years ago I began to take a more exact account than I had done before, of the manner wherein I spent my time, writing down how I had employed every hour. This I continued to do, wherever I was, till the time of my leaving England. The variety of scenes which I then passed through induced me to transcribe, from time to time, the more material parts of my diary, adding here and there such little reflections as occurred to my mind.

PREFACE TO JOURNAL, 1732

13

The nation is already involved in many troubles. And we know not how many more may follow. Are we able to extricate ourselves out of them all? If we have so much wisdom and strength that we need no help from man, are we quite sure that we need no help from God? I know your Lordship is not of that opinion. But if we need it, why are we ashamed to ask for it? To ask for it in the manner our forefathers did, in solemn public fasting and prayer? . . .

My Lord, my heart is full. Suffer me to speak; and if I speak as a fool, yet as a fool bear with me. Has your Lordship been ashamed (if every one else was) to mention this to His Majesty? Who besides your Lordship is likely to do it? Did prudence hinder you from doing it? . . . Now your Lordship has need of the whole armour of God . . . that you may answer the design of him who hath raised you up for this very thing, and placed you so near His Majesty that he might have one counsellor at least who dares not flatter but will speak the truth from his heart.

TO THE EARL OF DARTMOUTH, 1775

14

I am a Church-of-England man; and, as I said fifty years ago so I say still, in the Church I will live and die, unless I am thrust out.

·   ·   ·   ·   ·

Our glorying has been not to be a separate body.

TO HENRY MOORE, 1788

I have one point in view—to promote, so far as I am able, vital practical religion; and by the grace of God to beget, preserve and increase the life of God in the souls of men.

TO SAMUEL WALKER, 1756

15

My mother never would suffer one of her children to go to a dancing-school. But she had a dancing-master to come to her house who taught all of us what was sufficient in her presence. To this I have no objection. If I had convenience, I would be glad to have all our preachers taught, even by a dancing-master, to make a bow and to go in and out of a room.

TO JAMES BARRY, 1773

Of playing at cards, I say the same as of seeing plays, I could not do it with a clear conscience. But I am not obliged to pass any sentence on those that are otherwise minded.

THE MORE EXCELLENT WAY

16

Of all the seats of woe on this side hell few, I suppose, exceed or even equal Newgate. If any region of horror could exceed it a few years ago, Newgate in Bristol did; so great was the filth, the stench, the misery and wickedness which shocked all who had a spark of humanity left. How was I surprised, then, when I was there a few weeks ago! Every part of it, above stairs and below, even *the pit* wherein the felons are confined at night, is as clean and sweet as a gentleman's house. . . . The prison now has a new face; nothing offends either the eye or ear; and the whole has the appearance of a quiet, serious family. And does not the Keeper[1] of Newgate deserve to be remembered full as well as the Man of Ross?

TO THE LONDON CHRONICLE, 1761

[1]Abel Dagge.

17

Woman, remember the faith! In the name of God, set out again, and do the first works... Begin again without delay. The day after you receive this, go and meet a class or a band. Sick or well, go! If you cannot speak a word, go; and God will go with you. You sink under the sin of omission.

TO ANN BOLTON, 1790

I have been often musing upon this: Why the generality of Christians, even those that really are such, are less zealous and less active for God, when they are middle-aged than they were when they were young.

TO ELIZABETH RITCHIE, 1784

Fight on and conquer!

TO DOROTHY FURLY, 1757

18

There is no other religious Society under heaven which requires nothing of men in order to their admission into it, but a desire to save their souls. Look all around you, you cannot be admitted into the Church or Society of the Presbyterians, Anabaptists, Quakers, or any others, unless you hold the same opinions with them, and adhere to the same mode of worship. The Methodists alone do not insist on your holding this or that opinion, but they think and let think. Neither do they impose any particular mode of worship, but you may continue to worship in your former manner, be it what it may.

JOURNAL, 18th MAY 1788

19

I take knowledge, you are a young man; and as such, extremely
peremptory. So was I, till I was more than thirty years old. So I
may well make allowance for you. I was likewise as much
bigoted to my own opinions as you can be for your life; that is, I
thought them deeply important, and that all contrary opinions
were damnable errors. Have patience and you will see farther. In
a few years you will find out that neither these are half so
necessary to salvation, nor those half so destructive as you now
imagine.

.   .   .   .   .

Jealousy and suspiciousness I defy and abhor, as I do hell-fire.
And I believe nothing, great or small, without such kind of proof
as the nature of the thing allows.

TO SAMUEL FURLY, 1762

20

I was much concerned yesterday when I heard you were likely to
marry a woman against the consent of your parents. I have never
in an observation of fifty years known such a marriage attended
with a blessing. I know not how it should be, since it is flatly
contrary to the fifth commandment. I told my own mother, when
pressing me to marry: I dare not allow you a positive voice
herein; I dare not marry a person because you bid me. But I must
allow you a negative voice: I will marry no person if you forbid.
I know it would be a sin against God.'

TO ELIJAH BUSH, 1781

21

You know it is very natural for me to estimate wisdom and
goodness by years, and to suppose the longest experience must be

the best. But although there is much advantage in long experience, and we may trust an old soldier more than a novice; yet God is tied down to no rules; he frequently works a great work in a little time, he makes young men and women wiser than the aged, and gives to many in a very short time, a closer and deeper communion with himself than others attain in a long course of years.

TO MISS MARCH, 1774

22

When I was about twenty-two, my father pressed me to enter into holy orders. . . . I began to see that true religion was seated in the heart. . . . I began to alter the whole form of my conversation, and to set in earnest upon a new life. I set apart an hour or two a day for religious retirement. I communicated every week, I watched against all sin, whether in word or deed. I began to aim at, and pray for, inward holiness. So that now, doing so much, and living so good a life, I doubted not but I was a good Christian. . . .

I began to see more and more the value of time. I applied myself closer to study . . . I advised others to be religious. . . . The light flowed in so mightily upon my soul, that everything appeared in a new view.

JOURNAL, 24th MAY 1738

23

In this refined way of trusting to my own works and my own righteousness, I dragged on heavily, finding no comfort or help therein, till the time of my leaving England. On shipboard, however, I was again active in outward works; where it pleased God of his free mercy to give me twenty-six of the Moravian brethren for companions, who endeavoured to show me a more excellent way. But I understood it not at first. I was too learned and too wise. So that it seemed foolishness unto me. And I continued preaching, and following after, and trusting in, that righteousness whereby no flesh can be justified.

All the time I was at Savannah I was thus beating the air. . . . I sought to establish my own righteousness; and so laboured in the fire all my days.

JOURNAL, 24th MAY 1738

24

In the evening I went very unwillingly to a society in Aldersgate Street, where one was reading Luther's preface to the Epistle to the Romans. About a quarter before nine, while he was describing the change which God works in the heart through faith in Christ, I felt my heart strangely warmed. I felt I did trust in Christ, Christ alone for salvation; and an assurance was given me, that he had taken away *my* sins, even *mine*, and saved *me* from the law of sin and death.

I began to pray with all my might. . . . I then testified openly. . . . Then was I taught that peace and victory over sin are essential to faith in the Captain of our salvation.

JOURNAL, 24th MAY 1738

25

The moment I awaked, 'Jesus, Master,' was in my heart and in my mouth; and I found all my strength lay in keeping my eye fixed upon him, and my soul waiting on him continually. Being again at St. Paul's in the afternoon, I could taste the good word of God in the anthem: 'My song shall be always of the lovingkindness of the Lord; with my mouth will I ever be showing forth thy truth from one generation to another.'

.   .   .   .   .

All these days I scarce remember to have opened the Testament but upon some great and precious promise. And I saw more than ever, that the Gospel is in truth but one great promise from the beginning of it to the end.

JOURNAL, 25th MAY-4th JUNE 1738

26

Yet the enemy injected a fear: 'If thou dost believe, why is there not a more sensible change?' I answered (yet not I): 'That I know not. But this I know: I now have peace with God. And I sin not to-day, and Jesus has forbid me to take thought for the morrow.'

'But is not any sort of fear,' continued the tempter, 'a proof that thou dost not believe?' I desired my Master to answer for me, and opened his Book upon those words of St Paul: 'Without were fightings, within were fears.' Then, inferred I, well may fears be within me; but I must go on and tread them under my feet.

JOURNAL, 25th MAY 1738

27

Give me leave, my Lord, to say you have mistook and misrepresented this whole affair from the top to the bottom. And I am the more concerned to take notice of this because so many have fallen into the same mistake. It is indeed, and has been from the beginning, the capital blunder of our bitterest adversaries. . . . It is not our care, endeavour or desire to proselyte any from one man to another; or from one Church, from one congregation or Society, to another,—we would not move a finger to do this, to make ten thousand such proselytes,—but from darkness to light, from Belial to Christ, from the power of Satan to God. Our one aim is to proselyte sinners to repentance.

TO DR GIBSON, BISHOP OF LONDON, 1747

28

In the year 1729 four young students in Oxford agreed to spend their evenings together. They were all zealous members of the Church of England, and had no peculiar opinions, but were distinguished only by their constant attendance on the Church and Sacrament. In 1735 they were increased to fifteen, when the chief of them embarked for America, intending to preach to the heathen Indians. Methodism then seemed to die away; but it revived again in the year 1738, especially after Mr Wesley (not being allowed to preach in the Churches) began to preach in the fields.

THOUGHTS UPON METHODISM

29

In November, a large building, the Foundery, being offered him, he began preaching therein, morning and evening; at five in the morning, and seven in the evening, that the people's labour might not be hindered. From the beginning, the men and women sat apart, as they always did in the Primitive Church. And none were suffered to call any place their own, but the first comers sat down first. They had no pews; and all the benches for rich and poor, were of the same construction. Mr Wesley began the Service with a short prayer; then sung a hymn and preached (usually about half an hour), then sang a few verses of another hymn, and concluded with prayer. His constant doctrine was salvation by faith, preceded by repentance, and followed by holiness.

THOUGHTS UPON METHODISM

30

What was their fundamental doctrine? That the Bible is the whole and sole rule both of Christian faith and practice. Hence they learned, 1. That religion is an inward principle; that it is none other than the mind that was in Christ; or, in other words, the renewal of the soul after the image of God, in righteousness and true holiness; 2. That this can never be wrought in us, but by the power of the Holy Ghost, 3. That we receive this and every other blessing, merely for the sake of Christ; and, 4. That whosoever hath the mind that was in Christ, the same is our brother and sister and mother.

THOUGHTS UPON METHODISM

31

Who was the occasion of the Methodist preachers first setting foot in Leeds? William Shent.

Who was it that invited me and received me when I came? William Shent.

Who was it that stood by me while I preached in the street with stones flying on every side? William Shent.

Who was it that bore the storm of persecution for the whole town and stemmed it at the peril of his life? William Shent.

Whose word did God bless for many years in an eminent manner? William Shent's.

Who is he that is ready now to be broken up and turned into the street? William Shent.

And does nobody care for this? William Shent fell into sin and was publicly expelled the Society; but must he be also starved? ...Where is gratitude? Where is compassion? Where is Christianity? Where is humanity?... Let us set him on his feet once more.

TO THE SOCIETY AT KEIGHLEY, 1779

JUNE

1

Of all preaching, what is usually called Gospel preaching is the most useless, if not the most mischievous; a dull, yea or lively, harangue on the sufferings of Christ or salvation by faith without strongly inculcating holiness. I see more and more that this naturally tends to drive holiness out of the world.

TO CHARLES WESLEY, 1772

Do not lightly take the Name of God in your mouth; do not talk of the will of God on every trifling occasion.

THE NATURE OF ENTHUSIASM

2

I dare not insist upon anyone's using the word *Trinity* or *Person*. I use them myself without any scruple because I know of none better. But if any man has any scruple concerning them, who shall constrain him to use them? I cannot; much less would I burn a man alive, and that with moist green wood, for saying: 'Though I believe the Father is God, the Son is God, and the Holy Ghost is God, yet I scruple using the words *Trinity* and *Person* because I do not find those terms in the Bible.' . . . I would insist only on the direct words unexplained, just as they lie in the text: 'There are Three that bear record in Heaven, the Father, the Word, and the Holy Ghost; and these Three are One.'

THE TRINITY

3

You believe there is such a thing as *light,* whether flowing from the sun or any other luminous body. But you cannot comprehend either its nature or the manner wherein it flows. How does it move from Jupiter to the earth in eight minutes, two hundred thousand miles in a moment? How do the rays of the candle brought into the room instantly disperse into every corner? Here are three candles, yet there is but one light. Explain this, and I will explain the Three-One God.

The knowledge of the Three-One God is interwoven with all true Christian faith, with all vital religion.

THE TRINITY

4

Loyalty is with me an essential branch of religion, and which I am sorry any Methodist should forget. There is the closest connexion, therefore, between my religious and my political conduct. The selfsame authority enjoining me to fear God and to honour the King.

TO ELLIZABETH RITCHIE, 1777

The supposition that *the people* are the origin of power is every way indefensible.

THOUGHTS CONCERNING THE ORIGIN OF POWER

You will never see yourself aright, till he light his candle in your breast.

WORKS IX: 464

5

1. I always use a short, private prayer when I attend the public service of God...

2. I stand whenever I sing the praise of God in public...

3. I always kneel before the Lord my Maker when I pray in public.

4. I generally in public use the Lord's Prayer, because Christ has taught me, when I pray, to say: *Our Father.*

I advise every preacher connected with me, herein to tread in my steps.

JOURNAL, 5th JUNE 1766

6

The Methodists in general, my Lord, are members of the Church of England. They hold all her doctrines, attend her Service, and partake of her Sacraments.... For what reasonable end would your Lordship drive these people out of the Church? Are they not as quiet, as inoffensive, nay, as pious, as any of their neighbours, except perhaps here and there a hair-brained man who knows not what he is about?... Is it a Christian, yea, a Protestant Bishop, that so persecutes his own flock?

TO DR TOMLINE, BISHOP OF LINCOLN, 1790

7

It was from an ancient sect of physicians, whom we were supposed to resemble in our regular diet and exercise, that we were originally styled Methodists.... We were High Churchmen in the strongest sense. But we acknowledge as brethren all Dissenters, whether they are called Methodists or not.

TO DR FREE, 1758

I positively forbid you or any preacher to be a leader; rather put the most insignificant person in each class to be the leader of it.

TO JOHN CRICKET, 1783

It is right to add as much solemnity as we can to the admission of new members.

TO JOHN VALTON, 1783

8

Peter Jaco would willingly travel. But how? Can you help us to a horse that will carry him and his wife? What a pity we could not procure a camel or elephant!

TO CHRISTOPHER HOPPER, 1773

I must be on horseback for life, if I would be healthy. Now and then indeed, if I could afford it, I should rest myself for fifty miles in a chaise; but without riding near as much as I do now, I must never look for health.

TO EBENEZER BLACKWELL, 1764

9

God does not expect us to be sticks or stones. We may *grieve* and yet not murmur.

TO HIS NIECE, SARAH WESLEY, 1788

You have your hands full of business; but it will not hurt you while your heart is free.

TO ANN BOLTON, 1783

True religion has nothing sour, austere, unsociable, unfriendly in it.

TO MRS CHAPMAN, 1737

10

It is a bad dog that is not worth whistling for.

TO CHARLES WESLEY, 1786

A little well-placed raillery will often pierce deeper than solid argument.

THE DUTY OF REPROVING OUR NEIGHBOUR

Is there any fool or madman under heaven who can be compared to him that casts away his own soul, though it were to gain the whole world?

THE IMPORTANT QUESTION

Let the frog swell as long as he can, he will not equal the ox.

TO JOHN DOWNES, 1759

11

I have often thought of a saying of Dr Hayward's when he examined me for priest's orders: 'Do you know what you are about? You are bidding defiance to all mankind. He that would live a Christian priest ought to know that, whether his hand be against every man or no, he must expect every man's hand should be against him.' It is not strange that every man's hand who is not a Christian should be against him that endeavours to be so. But is it not hard that even those that are with us should be against us? That a man's enemies (in some degree) should be those of the same household of faith? Yet so it is. From the time that a man sets himself to his business, very many, even of those who travel the same road, many of those who are before as well as behind him, will lay stumbling-blocks in his way.

TO SAMUEL WESLEY, JUNE 1731

12

I allow that what is commonly called a religious education frequently does more hurt than good; and that many of the persons who were so educated are sinners above other men, and have contracted an enmity to religion which usually continues all their lives. And this will naturally be the case, if either the religion wherein they are instructed or the manner of instructing them be wrong. How few there are of those that undertake the education of children who understand the nature of religion, who know what true religion is!

THOUGHTS ON EDUCATION

13

When I had lived upwards of thirty years, I looked upon myself to stand just in the same relation to my father as I did when I was ten years old. And when I was between forty and fifty, I judged myself fully as much obliged to obey my mother in everything lawful, as I did when I was in my leading-strings.

.   .   .   .   .

Do nothing which you know your parents disapprove.

.   .   .   .   .

I call those cruel parents, who pass for kind and indulgent; who permit their children to contract habits which they know must be afterwards broken.

OBEDIENCE TO PARENTS

14

A true Protestant believes in God, has a full confidence in his mercy, fears him with a filial fear, and loves him with all his soul. He worships God in spirit and in truth; in everything gives him thanks; calls upon him with his heart as well as his lips at all times and in all places; honours his holy Name and his Word, and serves him truly all the days of his life.

TO A ROMAN CATHOLIC

15

In the evening I went to a Society at Wapping, weary in body and faint in spirit. I intended to speak on Romans 3^{19}, but could not tell how to open my mouth; and, all the time we were singing, my mind was full of some place, I knew not where, in the Epistle to the Hebrews. I begged God to direct, and opened the book on Hebrews 16^{19}: 'Having therefore, brethren, boldness to enter into the holiest by the blood of Jesus, by a new and living way, which he hath consecrated for us, through the veil, that is to say, his flesh,—let us draw near with a true heart in full assurance of faith, having our hearts sprinkled from an evil conscience, and our bodies washed with pure water.'

JOURNAL, 15th JUNE 1739

16

I impose my opinions upon none. . . . I make no opinion the term of union with any man; I think and let think. What I want is holiness of heart and life.

.   .   .   .   .

I desire to have a league offensive and defensive, with every soldier of Christ. We have not only one faith, one hope, one

Lord, but are directly engaged in one warfare. We are carrying the war into the devil's own quarters, who therefore summons all his hosts to war. Come then, ye that love him, to the help of the Lord against the mighty!

TO THE REV. J. VENN, 1763

17

I am glad you come a little nearer the good old Emperor's advice: 'Throw away that thirst for books.'[1] That thirst is the symptom of an evil disease; and 'his own indulgence makes the dreadful dropsy grow.'[2] What is the real value of a thing but the price it will bear in eternity! Let no study swallow up or entrench upon the hours of private prayer. Nothing is of so much importance. Simplify both religion and every part of learning as much as possible. Be all alive to God, and you will be useful to men.

TO JOSEPH BENSON, 1770

18

I advise you: (1) Be electrified (if need be) eight or ten times. (2) Keep your body always open, and that by food (as baked, boiled or roasted apples) rather than by physic. (3) Wash your head every morning with cold water, and rub it well with a coarse hempen towel. (4) I advise you and Sister Taylor to breakfast three or four weeks on nettle tea. Then you will find preaching, especially in the morning, one of the noblest medicines in the world.

TO THOMAS TAYLOR, 1775

---

[1] Marcus Aurelius.   [2] Horace.

19

This is my answer to them that trouble me, and will not let my grey hairs go down to the grave in peace. I am not a man of duplicity; I am not an old hypocrite, a double-tongued knave. . . . I have no temporal end to serve. I seek not the honour that cometh of men. It is not for pleasure that at this time of life I travel three or four thousand miles a year.

TO THE DUBLIN CHRONICLE, 1789

Leisure and I have taken leave of one another; I propose to be busy as long as I live, if my health is so long indulged to me. In health and sickness I hope I shall ever continue with the same sincerity.

TO HIS BROTHER SAMUEL, 1726

20

It is a stated rule in interpreting Scripture, never to depart from the plain, literal sense, unless it implies an absurdity.

THE CHURCH

On Scripture and common sense I build all my principles.

TO SAMUEL SPARROW, 1773

I must declare just what I find in the Book.

JOURNAL, 2nd NOVEMBER 1772

21

I have sometimes thought you are a little like me. My wife used to tell me: 'My dear, you are too generous. You don't know the value of money.' I could not wholly deny the charge. Possibly you may sometimes lean to the same extreme. I know you are of a generous spirit. You have an open heart and an open hand. But may it not sometimes be too open, more so than your circumstances will allow.

Is it not an instance of Christian (as well as worldly) prudence, to cut our coat according to our cloth? If your circumstances are a little narrower, should you not contract your expenses too? I need but just give you this hint, which I doubt not you will take kindly.

TO MRS CHARLES WESLEY, 1788

22

Can any man seriously think I despise learning who has ever heard of the school at Kingswood? especially if he knows with how much care and expense and labour I have kept it on foot for these twenty years? Let him but read the rules of Kingswood School, and he will urge this objection no more. . . .

I do not depreciate learning of any kind. The knowledge of the languages is a valuable talent, so is the knowledge of the arts and sciences. Both the one and the other may be employed to the glory of God and the good of man. But yet I ask, Where hath God declared in his Word that he cannot or will not make use of men that have it not? . . . You know the Apostles themselves, all except St. Paul, were common, unphilosophical, unlettered men.

TO DR THOMAS RUTHERFORD, 1768

23

As long as I live the people shall have no share in choosing either stewards or leaders among the Methodists. We have not and never had any such custom. We are no republicans, and never intend to be. It would be better for those that are so minded to go quietly away. I have been uniform both in doctrine and discipline

for above these fifty years; and it is a little too late for me to turn
into a new path now I am grey-headed.

TO JOHN MASON, 1790

24

I abhor the thought of giving to twenty men the power to place or
displace the preachers in their congregations. How would he then
dare to speak an unpleasing truth? And if he did, what would
become of him? This must never be the case, while I live, among
the Methodists. . . . The point must be carried for the Methodist
preachers now or never; and I alone can carry it; which I will,
God being my helper.

TO SAMUEL BRADBURN, 1782

Many years ago one informed me at London: 'The stewards
have discovered they are not *your* stewards, but the *people's,* and
are to direct, not be *directed* by you.' The next Sunday I let them
drop, and named seven other stewards.

No contentious person shall for the future meet in any Conference.
They may *dispute* elsewhere if they please.

TO THOMAS WRIDE, 1785

25

I know not that you have anything to do with fear. Your continual
prayer should be for faith and love. I admired a holy man in
France who, considering the state of one who was full of doubts
and fears, forbade him to think of his sins at all, and ordered him
to think only of the love of God in Christ. The fruit was, all his
fears vanished away, and he lived and died in the triumph of his
faith.

TO MARY BISHOP, 1770

You fear when no fear is.

TO ZACHARIAH YEWDALL, 1782

Do right and fear nothing.

TO WM HOLMES, 1788

26

How impossible it is for a man to see things right when he is angry? Does not passion blind the eyes of the understanding as smoke does the bodily eyes? And how little of the truth can we learn from those who see nothing but through a cloud? Correction must not be given in anger; if it be so, it will lose its effect on the child, who will think he is corrected, not because he has done a fault, but because the parent is angry.

THE DUTIES OF HUSBANDS AND WIVES

27

Without putting on spectacles (which, blessed be God, I do not wear) I can read a little Latin still.

IN FREEMAN'S JOURNAL, 1780

I can face the north wind at seventy-seven better than I could at seven and twenty.

TO SAMUEL BRADBURN, 1781

This is the last day of my seventy-eighth year; and (such is the power of God) I feel as if it were my twenty-eighth.

TO CHARLES WESLEY, 1781

I am half blind and half lame; but by the help of God I creep on still.

TO THOS GREATHEAD, 1791

28

I this day enter on my eighty-fifth year. And what cause have I to praise God as for a thousand spiritual blessings, so for bodily blessings also! How little have I suffered yet by 'the rush of numerous years.' It is true, I am not so agile as I was in times past; I do not run or walk so fast as I did. My sight is a little decayed. My left eye is grown dim and hardly serves me to read. I have daily some pain in the ball of my right eye, as also in my right temple (occasioned by a blow received some months since), and in my right shoulder and arm, which I impute partly to a sprain and partly to the rheumatism. I find likewise some decay in my memory. . . .

JOURNAL, 28th JUNE 1788

29

I find no decay in my hearing, smell, taste or appetite (though I want but a third part of the food I did once), nor do I feel any such thing as weariness, either in travelling or preaching. And I am not conscious of any decay in writing sermons, which I do as readily and, I believe, as correctly as ever.

To what cause can I impute this, that I am as I am? First, doubtless to the power of God, fitting me for the work to which I am called, as long as he pleases to continue me therein; and next, subordinately to this, to the prayers of His children.

JOURNAL, 28th JUNE 1788

30

You are at present one body. You act in concert with each other and by united counsels. And now is the time to consider what can be done in order to continue this union. Indeed, as long as I live there will be no great difficulty. I am, under God, a centre of union to all our travelling as well as local preachers. . . .

Those who desire or seek any earthly thing, whether honour, profit or ease, will not, cannot continue in the Connexion; it will not answer their design. Some of them, perhaps a fourth of the whole number, will secure preferment in the Church. Others will turn Independents, and get separate congregations.

TO THE TRAVELLING PREACHERS, 1769

JULY

1

On notice of my death, let all the preachers in England and Ireland repair to London within six weeks.

Let them seek God by solemn fasting and prayer. Let them draw up articles of agreement to be signed by those who choose to act in concert.

Let those be dismissed who do not choose it in the most friendly manner possible.

Let them choose by votes a committee of three, five or seven, each of whom is to be Moderator in his turn.

Let the Committee do what I do now; propose preachers to be tried, admitted or excluded; fix the place of each preacher for the ensuing year and the time of the next Conference.

TO THE TRAVELLING PREACHERS, 1769

2

What cause have we to bleed before the Lord this day, that have so long neglected this great and good work! That have been preachers so many years, and have done so little by personal instruction for the saving of men's souls! If we had but set on this work sooner, how many more might have been brought to Christ! And how much holier and happier might we have made our

Societies before now! And why might we not have done it sooner? There were many hindrances in the way; and so there are still, and always will be; but the greatest hindrance was in ourselves, in our dulness and littleness of faith and love.

MINUTES OF CONVERSATION, 1744

3

After all our preaching, many of our people are almost as ignorant as if they had never heard the Gospel. I study to speak as plainly as I can; yet I frequently meet with those who have been my hearers for many years, who know not whether Christ be God or man; or that infants have any original sin. And how few are there that know the nature of repentance, faith and holiness! Most of them have a sort of confidence that Christ will justify and save them, while the world has their hearts, and they live to themselves. And I have found, by experience, that one of these has learned more from an hour's close discourse than from ten years' public preaching.

MINUTES OF CONVERSATIONS, 1744

4

For what avails public preaching alone, though we could preach like angels?

I heard Dr Lupton say, my father, visiting one of his parishioners, who had never missed going to Church for forty years, then lying on his death-bed, asked him: 'Thomas, where do you think your soul will go?' 'Soul! Soul!' said Thomas. 'Yes, do you not know what your soul is?' 'Aye, surely,' said he, 'Why, it is a little bone in the back, that lives longer than the rest of the body.' So much Thomas had learned by constantly hearing sermons, yea, and exceedingly good sermons, for forty years!

MINUTES OF CONVERSATIONS, 1744

5

Be honest, not purloining, not secreting or privately keeping back anything for yourself; not taking, using, disposing or giving away the least thing belonging to your employer, without his leave, without his knowledge and consent first asked and obtained. To do otherwise is no better than plain theft and cuts off all pretensions to honesty. Equally dishonest it is to hurt or waste anything, or to let it be lost through your carelessness or negligence.

DIRECTIONS TO SERVANTS

What servants, journeymen, labourers, carpenters, bricklayers, do as they would be done by? Which of them does as much work as he can? Set him down for a knave that does not.

Who does as he would be done by, in buying and selling, particularly in selling horses? Write him knave that does not. And the Methodist knave is the worst of all knaves.

MINUTES OF CONVERSATIONS, 1744

6

Then many of the Methodists growing rich, became lovers of the present world. Next they married unawakened or half-awakened wives, and conversed with their relations. Hence, worldly prudence, maxims, customs, crept back upon them, producing more and more conformity to the world. Hence followed gross neglect of relative duties, especially education of children. And this is not easily cured by the Preachers.

MINUTES OF CONVERSATIONS, 1744

7

The greatest hindrances . . . you are to expect from the rich or cowardly or lazy Methodists. But regard them not, neither stewards, leaders nor people. Whenever the weather will permit, go out, in God's name, into the most public places, and call all to repent and believe the Gospel; every Sunday in particular.

Question: What may we reasonably expect to be God's design in raising up the preachers called Methodists?
Answer: To reform the nation, particularly the Church; to spread Scriptural holiness over the land.

MINUTES OF CONVERSATIONS, 1744

8

It is desired that all things be considered as in the immediate presence of God. That we may meet with a single eye, and as little children, who have everything to learn; that every point which is proposed may be examined to the foundation: that every person may speak freely whatever is in his heart; and that every question that arises may be thoroughly debated and settled. . . .

While we are conversing let us have an especial care to set God always before us. In the intermediate hours, let us redeem all the time we can for private exercises. Therein let us give ourselves to prayer for one another and for a blessing on this our labour.

MINUTES OF CONVERSATIONS, 1744

9

Question: Do you not entail a schism on the Church? i.e. is it not probable that your hearers, after your death, will be scattered into all sects and parties, or that they will form themselves into a distinct sect?
Answer: 1. We are persuaded the body of our hearers will, even after our death, remain in the Church, unless they be thrust out.

2. We believe, notwithstanding, either that they will be thrust out, or that they will leaven the whole Church.

3. We do, and will do, all we can to prevent those consequences which are supposed likely to happen after our death.

4. But we cannot, with a good conscience, neglect the present opportunity of saving souls while we live, for fear of consequences which may possibly or probably happen after we are dead.

MINUTES OF CONVERSATIONS, 1744

10

Gaining knowledge is a good thing; but saving souls is a better. . . . You will have abundant time for gaining other knowledge if you spend all your mornings therein. Only sleep not more than you need; talk not more than you need; and never be idle, nor triflingly employed. But if you can do but one, either following your studies or by instructing the ignorant, let your studies alone. I would throw by all the libraries in the world rather than be guilty of the perdition of one soul.

·   ·   ·   ·   ·

True, it is far easier to preach a good sermon than to instruct the ignorant in the principles of religion.

MINUTES OF CONVERSATIONS, 1744

11

Build all preaching-houses, if the ground will permit, in the octagon form. It is best for the voice, and, on many accounts more commodious than any other. Let the roof rise one-third of the breadth; this is the true proportion. Have windows and doors enough; and let all the windows be sashed, opening downward. Let there be no tub-pulpit, but a square projection, with a long seat behind. Let there be no backs to the seats, which should have aisles on each side, and be parted in the middle by a rail running along, to divide the men from the women.

MINUTES OF CONVERSATIONS, 1744

12

Which is the best general method of preaching?
    i. To invite. ii. To convince. iii. To offer Christ. iv. To build up; and to do this, in some measure, in every sermon.
    1. Be sure to begin and end, precisely at the time appointed.
    2. Endeavour to be serious, weighty and solemn in your whole deportment before the congregation.
    3. Always suit your subject to the audience.
    4. Choose the plainest texts you can.
    5. Take care not to ramble from your text, but keep close to it, and make out from it what you take in hand.
    6. Beware of allegorizing or spiritualizing too much.
    7. Take care of anything awkward or affected, either in your phrase, gesture or pronunciation.

MINUTES OF CONVERSATIONS, 1744

13

The sum is: Go into every house, in course, and teach every one therein, young and old, if they belong to us, to be Christians inwardly and outwardly.
    Make every particular plain to their understanding. Fix it in their memory. Write it on their heart. In order to this, there must be 'line upon line, precept upon precept.' I remember to have heard my father ask my mother: 'How could you have the patience to tell that blockhead the same thing twenty times over?' She answered: 'Why, if I had told him but nineteen times, I should

have lost all my labour.' What patience indeed, what love, what knowledge is requisite for this!

MINUTES OF CONVERSATIONS, 1744

14

Should our helpers follow trades?

This is an important question; therefore it will be proper to consider it thoroughly. The question is not whether they may occasionally work with their hands, as St Paul did; but whether it be proper for them to keep shop and follow merchandise. Of those who do so at present, it may be observed, they are unquestionably upright men; they are men of considerable gifts. We see the fruit of their labour, and they have a large share in the esteem and love of the people. All this pleads on their side, and cannot but give us a prejudice in their favour. . . . But where will it stop? If one preacher follow trade, so may twenty; so may every one. And if any of them trade a little, why not ever so much? Who can fix how far he should go? Therefore, we advise our brethren who have been concerned herein, to give up all, and attend to the one business.

MINUTES OF CONVERSATIONS, 1744

15

It is true, this cannot be done on a sudden; but it may between this and the next Conference. And even as to the drops that many have sold, if their wives sell them at home, well; but it is not proper for any preacher to hawk them about; it has a bad appearance; it does not suit well the dignity of his calling.

Two years after, it was agreed by all our brethren, that no preacher who will not relinquish his trade of buying and selling or of making and vending pills, drops, balsams or medicines of any kind, shall be considered as a travelling preacher any longer;

and that it shall be demanded of all those preachers who have traded in cloth, hardware, pills, drops, balsams or medicines of any kind, at the next Conference, whether they have entirely left it off or not.

MINUTES OF CONVERSATIONS, 1744

16

1. Be diligent. Never be unemployed a moment. Never be triflingly employed. Never while away time; neither spend any more at any place than is strictly necessary.

2. Be serious. Let your motto be: Holiness to the Lord. Avoid all lightness, jesting and foolish talking.

3. Converse sparingly and cautiously with women; particularly with young women in private.

4. Take no step toward marriage without first acquainting us with your design.

5. Believe evil of no one, unless you see it done, take heed how you credit it. Put the best construction on everything. You know the judge is always supposed to be on the prisoner's side.

RULES OF A HELPER

17

6. Speak evil of no one; else your word especially would eat as doth a canker. Keep your thoughts within your own breast till you come to the person concerned.

7. Tell every one what you think wrong in him, and that plainly, and as soon as may be, else it will fester in your heart. Make all haste to cast the fire out of your bosom.

8. Do not affect the gentleman. You have no more to do with this character than with that of a dancing-master. A preacher of the Gospel is the servant of all.

9. Be ashamed of nothing but sin; not of fetching wood (if

time permit), or of drawing water; not of cleaning your own shoes or your neighbour's.

RULES OF A HELPER

18

10. Be punctual. Do everything exactly at the time. And, in general, do not mend our rules, but keep them: not for wrath but for conscience' sake.

11. You have nothing to do but to save souls; therefore spend and be spent in this work. And go allways, not only to those that want you, but to those that want you most.

12. Act in all things, not according to your own will, but as a son in the Gospel; as such, it is your part to employ your time in the manner which we direct; partly in preaching and visiting from house to house; partly in reading, meditation and prayer. Above all, if you labour with us in our Lord's vineyard, it is needful that you should do that part of the work which we advise, at those times and places which we judge most for his glory.

RULES OF A HELPER

19

Do not rashly tear asunder the sacred ties which unite you to any Christian Society. . . . Take care how you rend the Body of Christ, by separating from your brethren. It is a thing evil in itself. It is a sore evil in its consequences.

Beware of countenancing or abetting any Parties in a Christian Society. Never encourage, much less cause, either by word or action, any division therein. . . . Leave off contention before it is meddled with; shun the very beginning of strife.

Happy is he that attains the character of a peacemaker in the Church of God.

SCHISM

20

The whole body of Roman Catholics define schism, a separation from the Church of Rome; and almost all our own writers define it, a separation from the Church of England. Thus both the one and the other set out wrong and stumble at the very threshold....

The immense pains which have been taken both by Papists and Protestants in writing whole volumes against schism as a separation whether from the Church of Rome or from the Church of England, have been employed to mighty little purpose. They have been fighting with shadows of their own raising.

SCHISM

21

I have spoken the more explicitly upon this head because it is so little understood; because so many of those who profess much religion, nay, and really enjoy a measure of it, have not the least conception of this matter, neither imagine such a separation to be any sin at all. They leave a Christian Society with as much unconcern as they would go out of one room into another. They give occasion to all this complicated mischief; and wipe their mouth, and say they have done no evil! Whereas they are justly chargeable before God and man, both with an action that is evil in itself, and with all the evil consequences which may be expected to follow, to themselves, to their brethren and to the world.

SCHISM

22

In like manner, if I could not continue united to any smaller Society, Church or body of Christians, without committing sin, without lying and hypocrisy, without preaching to others doctrines which I did not myself believe, I should be under an absolute necessity of separating from that Society. And in all these cases the sin of separation, with all the evils consequent upon it, would not lie upon me, but upon those who constrained me to make that separation, by requiring of me such terms of communion as I could not in conscience comply with. But setting aside this case, suppose the Church or Society to which I am now united, does not require me to do anything which the Scripture forbids, or to omit anything which the Scripture enjoins, it is then my indispensable duty to continue therein.

SCHISM

23

I am now, and have been from my youth, a member and minister of the Church of England. And I have no desire nor design to separate from it till my soul separates from my body. Yet if I were not permitted to remain therein without omitting what God requires me to do, it would then become meet and right and my bounden duty to separate from it without delay. To be more particular, I know God has committed to me a dispensation of the Gospel. Yea, and my own salvation depends upon preaching it. 'Woe is me if I preach not the Gospel.' If then I could not remain in the Church without omitting this, without desisting from preaching the Gospel, I should be under the necessity of separating from it or losing my own soul.

SCHISM

24

A loving word, spoken in faith, shall not fall to the ground.

.   .   .   .   .

You have this treasure in an earthen vessel; you dwell in a poor shattered house of clay, which presses down the immortal spirit.

.   .   .   .   .

The knowledge of ourselves is true humility; and without this we cannot be freed from vanity.

.   .   .   .   .

It is a great thing to spend all our time to the glory of God.

TO MISS MARCH, 1760-77

25

I went to a gentleman who is much troubled with what they call lowness of spirits. Many such have I been with before; but in several of them it was no bodily distemper. They wanted something, they knew not what; and were therefore heavy, uneasy, and dissatisfied with everything. The plain truth is, they wanted God, they wanted Christ, they wanted faith; and God convinced them of their want, in a way their physicians no more understood than themselves. Accordingly nothing availed till the great Physician came. For in spite of all natural means, he who made them for himself would not suffer them to rest till they rested in him.

JOURNAL, 13th JULY 1739

26

Lord King's *Account of the Primitive Church* convinced me many years ago that bishops and presbyters are the same order, and consequently have the same right to ordain. For many years I have been importuned from time to time to exercise this right, by ordaining part of our travelling preachers. But I have still refused; not only for peace' sake, but because I was determined as little as possible to violate the established order of the national Church to which I belonged.

But the case is widely different between England and North America. Here there are bishops who have a legal jurisdiction. In America there are none, neither any parish ministers. So that for some hundred miles together there is none either to baptise or administer the Lord's Supper.

TO AMERICAN METHODISTS, 1784

27

Here therefore my scruples are at an end, and I conceive myself at full liberty, as I violate no order and invade no man's right, by appointing and sending labourers into the harvest. . . . And I have prepared a liturgy, little differing from that of the Church of England (I think the best constituted national Church in the world) which I advise all the travelling preachers to use on the Lord's Day, in all the congregations, reading the Litany only on Wednesdays and Fridays, and praying extempore on all other days. I also advise the elders to administer the Supper of the Lord on every Lord's Day.

If any one will point out a more rational and scriptural way of feeding and guiding those poor sheep in the wilderness, I will gladly embrace it.

TO AMERICAN METHODISTS, 1784

28

By this time I should be some judge of man; and if I am, all England and Ireland cannot afford such a body of men, number for number, for sense and true experience both of men and things, as the body of Methodist preachers. Our leaders in London, Bristol and Dublin are by no means weak men. I would not be ashamed to compare them with a like number of tradesmen in every part of the three kingdoms. But I assure you they are no more than children compared to the preachers in Conference, as you would be thoroughly convinced could you but have the opportunity of spending one day among them.

TO ALEXANDER CLARK, 1772

29

The Service of the Roman Church is everywhere performed in the Latin tongue, which is nowhere vulgarly understood . . . This irrational and unscriptural practice destroys the great end of public worship.

.   .   .   .   .

Scripture and antiquity are flatly against transubstantiation. And so are our very senses.

POPERY CALMLY CONSIDERED

The Church of Rome does not scruple to impose upon the consciences of men, in the doctrine of the Mass, various traditions, that have no authority in holy writ.

THE ADVANTAGE OF THE CHURCH OF ENGLAND

30

Is not Rome the mother of all Churches? We answer, No. The word of the Lord went forth from Jerusalem. There the Church began. She therefore, not the Church of Rome, is the mother of all Churches. The Church of Rome, therefore, has no right to require any person to believe what she teaches on her sole authority.

.   .   .   .   .

The Church of Rome is no more the Church in general than the Church of England is. It is only one particular branch of the Catholic or Universal Church of Christ, which is the whole body of believers in Christ, scattered over the whole earth. . . . In all cases, the Church is to be judged by the Scripture, not the Scripture by the Church.

POPERY CALMLY CONSIDERED

31

We grant confession to men to be, in many cases, of use, public in case of public scandal; private to a spiritual guide for disburdening of the conscience, and as a help to repentance. But to make auricular confession or particular confession to a priest necessary to forgiveness and salvation, when God has not so made it, is apparently to teach for doctrine the commandment of men; and to make it necessary in all cases is to make of what may be a useful means, a dangerous snare, both to the confessor and those that confess.

.   .   .   .   .

To pardon sin, and absolve the sinner judicially, so as the conscience may rest firmly upon it, is a power reserved by God to himself.

REPLY TO THE ROMAN CATECHISM

AUGUST

1

The greatest abuse of all in the Lord's Supper is the worshipping of the consecrated bread. And this the Church of Rome not only practises, but positively enjoins.

. . . . .

A more dangerous error in the Church of Rome is the forbidding the clergy to marry. . . . The Apostle, on the contrary, says: 'Marriage is honourable in all.'

. . . . .

Lastly, what can more directly tend to destroy truth from off the earth, than the doctrine of the Church of Rome that 'no faith is to be kept with heretics'?

POPERY CALMLY CONSIDERED

2

An evil practice is the depriving the laity of the Cup in the Lord's Supper. It is acknowledged by all that our Lord instituted and delivered this Sacrament *in both kinds,* giving the wine as well as the bread to all that partook of it, and that it continued to be so delivered in the Church of Rome for above a thousand years. And yet, notwithstanding this, the Church of Rome now forbids the people to *drink of the Cup*. A more insolent and barefaced corruption cannot easily be conceived.

Another evil practice in the Church of Rome, utterly unheard of in the ancient Church, is that when there is none to receive the Lord's Supper, the priest communicates alone. (Indeed, it is not properly to *communicate,* when only one receives it.) This likewise is an absolute innovation in the Church of God.

POPERY CALMLY CONSIDERED

3

My dear Friend, Consider, I am not persuading you to leave or change your religion, but to follow after that fear and love of God without which all religion is vain. I say not a word to you about your opinions or outward manner of worship; but I say all worship is an abomination to the Lord unless you worship him in spirit and in truth, with your heart as well as your lips, with your spirit and your understanding also. . . .

We ought, without this endless jangling about opinions, to provoke one another to love and to good works. Let the points wherein we differ stand aside; here are enough wherein we agree, enough to be the ground of every Christian temper and of every Christian action.

TO A ROMAN CATHOLIC

4

It is a known principle of the Church of England that nothing is to be received as an article of faith, which is not read in the holy Scripture or to be inferred therefrom, by just and plain consequences.

.   .   .   .   .

I lay this down as an undoubted truth: the more the doctrine of any Church agrees with the Scripture, the more readily ought it to be received. And on the other hand, the more the doctrine of any Church differs from the Scripture, the greater cause we have to doubt of it.

THE ADVANTAGE OF THE CHURCH OF ENGLAND

5

We honour the blessed Virgin as the Mother of the holy Jesus, and as she was a person of eminent piety; but we do not think it lawful to give that honour to her which belongs not to a creature and doth equal her with her Redeemer...We read nothing in the Bible of her bodily assumption into heaven nor of her exaltation to a throne above angels and archangels.

.   .   .   .   .

We freely own that Christ is to be adored in the Lord's Supper; but that the elements are to be adored, we deny.

REPLY TO THE ROMAN CATECHISM

6

As to my own judgment, I still believe the episcopal form of Church government to be both scriptural and apostolical, I mean, well agreeing with the practice and writings of the Apostles. But that it is *prescribed* in Scripture, I do not believe. This opinion, which I once zealously espoused, I have been heartily ashamed of, ever since I read Bishop Stillingfleet's *Irenicon*. I think he has unanswerably proved that neither Christ nor his Apostles *prescribe* any particular form of Church government, and that the plea of divine right for diocesan episcopacy was never heard of in the Primitive Church.

TO THE REV. JAMES CLARKE, 1756

7

I firmly believe I am a scriptural *episcopos* as much as any man in England or in Europe. For the Uninterrupted Succession I know to be a fable which no man ever did or can prove. . . .

I submit still (though sometimes with a doubting conscience) to Mitred Infidels. I do indeed vary from them in some points of doctrine and in some points of discipline: (by preaching abroad, for instance, by praying extempore, and by forming Societies.) But not a hair's breadth further than I believe to be meet, right and my bounden duty. I walk still by the same rule I have done for between forty and fifty years. I do nothing rashly. It is not likely I should. The high day of my blood is over.

SEPARATION FROM THE CHURCH

8

From a child I was taught to love and reverence the Scriptures, the Oracles of God; and next to these, to esteem the Primitive Fathers, the Writers of the first three centuries. Next after the Primitive Church, I esteemed our own, the Church of England, as the most scriptural national Church in the world. I therefore, not only assented to all the doctrines, but observed all the rubric in the Liturgy; and that with all possible exactness.

In this judgment, and with this spirit, I went to America, strongly attached to the Bible, the Primitive Church, and the Church of England, from which I would not vary in one jot or tittle on any account whatever. In this spirit I returned as regular a clergyman as any in the three kingdoms; till after not being permitted to preach in the Churches, I was constrained to *preach in the open air.*

SEPARATION FROM THE CHURCH

9

Here was my first *irregularity,* And it was not voluntary but constrained. The second was *extemporary* prayer. This likewise I believed to be my bounden duty, for the sake of those who desired me to watch over their souls. I could not in conscience refrain from it.

When the people joined together, simply to help each other to heaven, increased by hundreds and thousands, still they had no more thought of leaving the Church than of leaving the kingdom. Nay, I continually and earnestly cautioned them against it; reminding them that we were a part of the Church of England.

SEPARATION FROM THE CHURCH

10

1. Our design is, with God's assistance, to train up children in all such things as are needful for them.

2. We take them in between the ages of Six and Twelve in order to teach them Reading, Writing and Sewing; and, if it be desired, the English Grammar, Arithmetic & other Sorts of Needlework.

3. It is our particular Desire, that all who are educated here, may be brought up in the fear of God; And at the utmost distance as from Vice in general, so in particular from Idleness & Effeminacy. The Children therefore of tender parents so call'd (who are indeed offering up their Sons and their Daughters unto Devils) have no Business here: for the rules will not be broken in favour of any person whatsoever. Nor is any Child received unless her Parents agree, 1. That she shall observe all the Rules of the House, & 2. That they will not take her from School, no, not a Day, till they take her for good and all.

RULES FOR THE GIRLS' SCHOOL AT KINGSWOOD

11

Why are we more nervous than our forefathers? Because we lie longer in bed; they, rich and poor, slept about eight, when they heard the curfew bell, and rose at four; the bell ringing at that hour (as well as at eight) in every parish in England. . . .

Yet something may be allowed to irregular passions for these undoubtedly affect the body, the nerves in particular. Even violent joy, though it raises the spirits for a time, does afterwards sink them greatly. And every one knows what an influence fear has upon our whole frame. Nay, even hope deferred maketh the heart grow sick, puts the mind all out of tune. The same effect have all foolish and hurtful desires. They pierce us through with many sorrows.

THOUGHTS ON NERVOUS DISORDERS

12

Is there no remedy for lowness of spirits? Undoubtedly there is, a most certain cure, if you are willing to pay the price of it. But this price is not silver or gold, nor anything purchasable thereby. If you would give all the substance of your house for it, it would be utterly despised. And all the medicines under the sun avail nothing in this distemper. The whole *Materia Medica* put together will do you no lasting service; they do not strike at the root of the disease; you must remove the cause, if you wish to remove the effect. But this cannot be done by your own strength; it can only be done by the mighty power of God. If you are convinced of this, set about it trusting in him, and you will surely conquer.

THOUGHTS ON NERVOUS DISORDERS

13

Abstain from all spirituous liquors. Touch them not on any pretence whatever.

.   .   .   .   .

Every day of your life take at least an hour's exercise . . . If you can, take it in the open air.

.   .   .   .   .

Sleep early and rise early, unless you are ill.

.   .   .   .   .

Beware of anger! Beware of worldly sorrow! Beware of the fear that hath torment! Beware of foolish and hurtful desires! Beware of inordinate affection! Remember the command: 'My son, give me thy heart!'

THOUGHTS ON NERVOUS DISORDERS

14

There is, indeed, a wide difference between the relation wherein you stand to the Americans and the relation wherein I stand to all the Methodists. . . . I am under God the father of the whole family. Therefore I naturally care for you all in a manner no other persons can do. Therefore I in a measure provide for you all . . .

But in one point, my dear brother, I am a little afraid both the Doctor[1] and you differ from me. I study to be little: you study to be great. I creep: you strut along. I found a school: you a college! Nay, and call it after you own names! . . .

One instance of this has given me great concern. How can you, how dare you suffer yourself to be called Bishop? I shudder, I start at the very thought! Men may call me a knave or a fool, a

[1]Dr. Coke.

rascal, a scoundrel, and I am content; but they shall never by my consent call me Bishop!

TO FRANCIS ASBURY, 1788

15

You were never in your lives in so critical a situation as you are at this time. It is your part to be peacemakers, to be loving and tender to all, but to addict yourselves to no party. In spite of all solicitations, of rough or smooth words, say not one word against one or the other side. Keep yourselves pure, do all you can to help and soften all; but beware how you adopt another's war.

See that you act in full union with each other; this is of the utmost consequence. Not only let there be no bitterness or anger but no shyness or coldness between you.

TO THE PREACHERS IN AMERICA, 1775

16

They [the Methodists] have many schools for teaching, reading, writing and arithmetic, but only one for teaching the higher parts of learning. This is kept in Kingswood, near Bristol, and contains about forty scholars.

. . . . .

Each preacher has his food wherever he labours and twelve pounds a year for clothes and other expenses. If he is married, he has ten pounds a year for his wife. This money is raised by the voluntary contributions of the Societies. It is by these likewise that the poor are assisted where the allowance fixed by the laws of the land does not suffice. Accordingly the stewards of the Societies in London distribute seven or eight pounds weekly among the poor.

. . . . .

There are only three Methodist Societies in America. . . . There are five preachers there.

TO PROFESSOR JOHN LIDEN OF LUND, 1769

17

How can it enter into the thoughts of man that the soul, which is capable of such immense perfections and of receiving new improvements to all eternity, shall fall away into nothing almost as soon as it is created? Are such abilities made for no purpose?

The silkworm, after having spun her task, lays her eggs and dies. But a man can never have taken in his full measure of knowledge, has not time to subdue his passions, establish his soul in virtue, and come up to the perfection of his nature, before he is hurried off the stage. Would an infinitely wise Being make such glorious beings for so mean a purpose? Can he delight in the production of such abortive intelligences? . . . Would he give us talents that are not to be exerted, capacities that are never to be gratified?

THE IMMORTALITY OF THE SOUL

18

How can we find that wisdom that shines through all his works, in the formation of man, without looking on this world as only a nursery for the next, and believing that the several generations of rational creatures, which rise up and disappear in such quick successions, are only to receive their first rudiments of existence here, and afterwards to be translated into a more friendly climate, where they may spread and flourish to all eternity?

.   .   .   .   .

With what astonishment and veneration may we look into our souls where there are such hidden stores of virtue and knowledge!

Such inexhausted sources of perfection! We know not yet what we shall be, nor will it ever enter into the heart of man to conceive the glory that will be always in reserve for him.

THE IMMORTALITY OF THE SOUL

19

Nor is it expedient for any Methodist preacher to imitate the Dissenters in their manner of praying, either in his tone: all particular tones both in prayer and preaching should be avoided with the utmost care; nor in his language: all his words should be plain and simple, such as the lowest of his hearers both use and understand; or in the length of his prayer which should not usually exceed four or five minutes, either before or after sermon. One might add, neither should we sing like them in a slow, drawling manner; we sing swift, both because it saves time, and because it tends to awake and enliven the soul.

REASONS AGAINST A SEPARATION FROM THE
CHURCH OF ENGLAND

20

Persecution never did, never could give any lasting wound to genuine Christianity. But the greatest it ever received, the grand blow which was struck at the very root of that humble, gentle, patient love, which is the fulfilling of the Christian law, the whole essence of true religion, was struck in the fourth century by Constantine the Great, when he called himself a Christian, and poured in a flood of riches, honours and power upon the Christians, more especially upon the clergy. . . . Then not the golden but the iron age of the Church commenced. . . . And this is the event which most Christian expositors mention with such triumph!

THE MYSTERY OF INIQUITY

21

All matter indeed is continually changing, and that into ten thousand forms. But that it is changeable does in no wise imply that it is perishable. The substance may remain one and the same, though under innumerable different forms. It is very possible any portion of matter may be resolved into the atoms of which it was originally composed. But what reason have we to believe that one of those atoms ever was or ever will be annihilated?

It is a vain thought which some have entertained, that death will put an end to the soul as well as the body. It will put an end to neither the one nor the other; it will only alter the manner of their existence.

THE ETERNITY OF GOD

22

It is true believers may not all speak alike; they may not all use the same language. It is not to be expected that they should; we cannot reasonably require it of them. A thousand circumstances may cause them to vary from each other in the matter of expressing themselves. But a difference of expression does not necessarily imply a difference of sentiment. Different persons may use different expressions and yet mean the same thing.

Men may differ from us in their opinions, as well as their expressions, and nevertheless be partakers with us of the same precious faith.

THE LORD OUR RIGHTEOUSNESS

23

Persons may be quite right in their opinions and yet have no religion at all. And, on the other hand, persons may be truly religious who hold many wrong opinions.

.   .   .   .   .

There are ten thousand mistakes which may consist with real religion, with regard to which every candid, considerate man will think and let think. But there are some truths more important than others.

THE TRINITY

Where is our religion, if we cannot think and let think?

.   .   .   .   .

As we have one Lord, one Faith, one Hope of our calling, let us all strengthen each other's hands in God.

THE LORD OUR RIGHTEOUSNESS

24

I must entreat you, in the Name of God, be open to conviction. Whatever prejudices you have contracted from education, custom, or example, divest yourselves of them, as far as possible. Be willing to receive light either from God or man; do not shut your eyes against it. Rather be glad to see more than you did before, to have the eyes of your understanding opened.

.   .   .   .   .

You who have passed the morning, perhaps the noon of life, who find the shadows of the evening approach, set a better example to those that are to come, to the now-rising generation. . . . See that you redeem every moment that remains.

ADVICE WITH REGARD TO DRESS

25

Can anything be more absurd than for men to cry out: 'The Church! The Church!' and to pretend to be very zealous for it and violent defenders of it, while they themselves have neither part nor lot therein, nor indeed, know what the Church is?

THE CHURCH

I am not afraid that the people called Methodists should ever cease to exist either in Europe or America: but I am afraid lest they should only exist as a dead sect, having the form of religion without the power. And this undoubtedly will be the case unless they hold fast both the doctrine, spirit and discipline with which they first set out.

THOUGHTS UPON METHODISM

26

When you despise or depreciate reason, you must not imagine you are doing God service; least of all, are you promoting the cause of God, when you are endeavouring to exclude reason out of religion. Unless you wilfully shut your eyes, you cannot but see of what service it is both in laying the foundation of true religion, under the guidance of the Spirit of God, and in raising the superstructure. You see, it directs us in every point, both of faith and practice; it guides us with regard to every branch both of inward and outward holiness. Do we not glory in this, that the whole of our religion is a *reasonable service*?

THE CASE OF REASON

27

Permit me to add a few plain words to you likewise who overvalue reason. Why should you roam from one extreme to the other? Is not the middle way best? Let reason do all that reason can; employ it as far as it will go. But, at the same time, acknowledge it is utterly incapable of giving either faith, hope or love, and, consequently of producing either real virtue or substantial happiness. Expect these from a higher source, even from the Father of the spirits of all flesh. Seek and receive them, not as your own acquisition, but as the gift of God.

THE CASE OF REASON

28

As I have made a beginning, as the men and women are already separated in the Chapel at Manchester, I beg that Brother Brocklehurst and you will resolutely continue that separation. This is a Methodist rule, not grounded on caprice, but on plain, solid reason; and it has been observed at Manchester for several years; neither upon the whole have we lost anything thereby. By admitting the contrary practice, by jumbling men and women together, you would shut *me* out of the house: for if I should come into a Methodist preaching when this is the case, I must immediately go out again. But I hope this will never be the case.

TO JOHN VALTON, 1781

29

Let every one speak as he finds; as for me, I cannot admire either the wisdom or virtue or happiness of mankind. Wherever I have been, I have found the bulk of mankind, Christian as well as heathen, deplorably ignorant, vicious and miserable.... Sin and pain are on every side. And who can account for this but on the supposition that we are in a fallen state?... Yet none need perish; for we have an almighty Saviour.

TO SAMUEL SPARROW, 1773

30

Is it not the common practice of the old men to praise the past and condemn the present? And this may probably operate much further than one would at first imagine. When those that have more experience than we, and therefore, we are apt to think, more wisdom, are almost continually harping upon this, the degeneracy of the world, is it any wonder if, being accustomed from our infancy to hear how much better the world was formerly than it is now, (and so it really seemed to them, when they were young, and when the cheerfulness of youth gave a pleasing air to all that was around them,) the idea of the world's being worse and worse should naturally grow up with us? And so it will till we, in our turn, grow peevish, fretful, discontented, and full of melancholy complaints: 'How wicked the world is grown! How much better it was when we were young, in the golden days that we can remember!'

FORMER TIMES

31

This world is a world of mercy wherein God pours down many mercies, even on the evil and the unthankful. And many of these, it is very probable, are conveyed even to them by the ministry of angels.

GOOD ANGELS

Next to the love of God, there is nothing which Satan so cordially abhors as the love of our neighbour. He uses therefore every possible means to prevent or destroy this; to excite either private or public suspicions, animosities, resentment, quarrels; to destroy the peace of families or of nations, and to banish unity and concord from the earth. And this, indeed, is the triumph of his art: to embitter the children of men against each other, and, at length, to urge them to do his own work, to plunge one another into the pit of destruction. . . . He is equally diligent to hinder every good word and work. . . . He strives to instil unbelief, atheism, illwill.

EVIL ANGELS

SEPTEMBER

1

It is true in some things we vary from the rule of our Church, but no further than we apprehend is our bounden duty. It is upon a full conviction of this that we preach abroad, use extemporary prayer, form those who appear to be awakened into Societies, and permit laymen, whom we believe God has called, to preach.

TO THOMAS ADAM, 1755

I would observe every punctilio of order, except where the salvation of souls is at stake. There I prefer the end before the means.

TO THE REV. GEORGE DOWNING, 1761

2

Why should any man of reason and religion be either afraid of, or averse to salvation from all sin? Is not sin the greatest evil on this side hell? And if so, does it not naturally follow that an entire deliverance from it is one of the greatest blessings on this side Heaven?

.   .   .   .   .

In God's Name, why are you so fond of sin? What good has it ever done you? What good is it ever likely to do you, either in this world or in the world to come? And why are you so violent against those that hope for a deliverance from it? Have patience with us.

PERFECTION

3

You oblige me by speaking your sentiments so plainly: with the same plainness I will answer. So far as I know myself, I have no more concern for the reputation of Methodism or my own than for the reputation of Prester John. I have the same point in view as when I set out—the promoting as I am able vital, practical religion; and in all our discipline I still aim at the continuance of the work which God has already begun in so many souls. With this view, and this only, I permitted those whom I believed God had called thereto to comfort, exhort and instruct their brethren. And if this end can be better answered some other way, I shall subscribe to it without delay.

TO THE REV. SAMUEL WALKER, 1756

4

You will have no blessing from God and no praise from wise men if you take that vile sordid measure (especially at this time!) of so reducing the salary. You *must* give £40 a year at the least. . . .

I abhor the thought of our master's keeping an evening school. It would swallow up the time he ought to have for his own improvement. Give him enough to live comfortably upon without this drudgery.

TO ARTHUR KEENE, 1785

Throughout England, Wales and Ireland each of our preachers has three pounds a quarter.

TO SARAH BAKER, 1784

5

I have *two* silver teaspoons at London, and *two* at Bristol. This is all the plate which I have at present; and I shall not buy any more while so many round me want bread.

TO THE OFFICER OF EXCISE, 1776

Gentlemen—Two or three days ago Mr Ireland sent me as a present two dozen of French claret, which I am ordered to drink during my present weakness. At the White Swan it was seized. Beg it may be restored to your obedient servant, John Wesley. Whatever duty comes due I will see duly paid.

TO THE CUSTOM HOUSE, 1790

6

Cheerfulness is a great blessing.

TO MRS ARMSTRONG, 1790

One good temper is of more value in the sight of God than a thousand good verses.

TO AGNES COLLINSON, 1788

Make the best of life.

TO HIS NIECE, SARAH WESLEY, 1788

Every believer ought to *enjoy* life.

TO SAMUEL BRADBURN, 1787

7

I do not see how it is possible, in the nature of things, for any revival of true religion to continue long; for religion must

necessarily produce both industry and frugality, and these cannot
but produce riches; but as riches increase, so will pride, anger,
and love of the world in all its branches.

THOUGHTS UPON METHODISM

It is a sad observation that they that have most money have
usually least grace.

TO FREEBORN GARRETTSON, 1785

8

We purpose to consider fully at the Conference the state of our
brethren in America, and to send them all the help we can both in
Nova Scotia and in other parts. But whoever goes over must
voluntarily offer himself for that great work. I not only do not
require but do not so much as advise any one to go. His service
will do no good there unless it be a freewill offering.

TO ALEXANDER BARRY, 1784

9

You are in a large way of business, wherein I suppose you clear
one (if not two or three) hundred a year. Over and above that you
have an estate which, if you gave above thirty years' purchase, is
a hundred a year. You have neither son nor daughter; and yet you
cannot afford sixpence a month for the *Magazine*! Nay, you could
not afford to give a guinea in a pressing case, viz. at the instance
of an old tried friend! . . . I do not know that in forty years I have
asked a guinea of any other man that has denied me!

TO WILLIAM ROBARTS, 1782

Is it fit for me to ask a Methodist *twice* for anything in his power.

TO MRS BOWMAN, 1789

10

If you fall upon people that meddle not with you, without either fear or wit, you may possibly find they have a little more to say for themselves than you are aware of. I follow peace with all men; but if a man set upon me without either rhyme or reason, I think it my duty to defend myself so far as truth and justice permit.

TO THE REV. JOHN DOWNES, 1759

Near fifty years ago, a great and good man, Dr. Potter, then Archbishop of Canterbury, gave me an advice for which I have ever since had occasion to bless God; 'If you desire to be extensively useful, do not spend your time and strength in contending for or against such things as are of a disputable nature; but in testifying against notorious vice, and in promoting essential holiness.'

ATTENDING THE CHURCH SERVICE

11

Many years ago when one was describing the glorious privilege of a believer, I cried out: 'If this be so, I have no faith.' He replied: 'You have faith, but it is weak.' The very same thing I say to you, my dear friend. You have faith, but it is only as a grain of mustard seed. Hold fast what you have, and ask for what you want. There is an irreconcilable variability in the operations of the Holy Spirit on the souls of men, more especially as to the manner of justification. Many find him rushing upon them like a torrent, while they experience 'the overwhelming power of saving grace.' This has been the experience of many . . . But in others he works in a very different way, in a gentle and almost insensible manner. Let him take his own way. He is wiser than you. He will do all things well.

TO MARY COOKE, 1785

12

We may go through abundance of business, and yet have God in all our thoughts. . . . In this respect, as in many others, I have lately had peculiar reason to be thankful. In every place people flock about me for direction in secular as well as spiritual affairs; and I dare not throw even this burden off my shoulders, though I have employment enough without it. But it is a burden, and no burden; it is no encumbrance, no weight upon my mind. If we see God in all things and do all for him, then all things are easy.

TO EBENEZER BLACKWELL, 1757

13

Though I am always in haste, I am never in a hurry, because I never undertake any more work than I can go through with perfect calmness of spirit. It is true I travel four or five thousand miles in a year. But I generally travel alone in my carriage, and consequently am as retired ten hours in a day as if I were in a wilderness. On other days, I never spend less than three hours (frequently ten or twelve) in the day alone. So there are few persons in the kingdom who spend so many hours secluded from all company. Yet I find time to visit the sick and the poor. . . . When I was at Oxford, and lived almost like a hermit, I saw not how any busy man could be saved. I scarcely thought it possible for a man to retain the Christian spirit amidst the noise and bustle of the world. God taught me better by my own experience. I had ten times more business in America (that is, at intervals) than ever I had in my life. But it was no hindrance to silence of spirit.

TO MISS MARCH, 1777

14

Two and forty years ago, having a desire to furnish poor people with cheaper, shorter and plainer books than any I had seen, I wrote many small tracts, generally a penny a-piece; and afterwards several larger. Some of these had such a sale as I never thought of; and, by this means, I unawares became rich. But I never desired or endeavoured after it. And now that it is come upon me unawares, I lay up no treasures upon earth: I lay up nothing at all. . . . I cannot help leaving my books behind me whenever God calls me hence; but, in every other respect, my own hands will be my executors.

THE DANGER OF RICHES

15

We may suppose that your sons have now been long enough at School, and you are thinking of some business for them. Before you determine anything on this head, see that your eye be single. Is it so? Is it your view to please God herein? It is well if you take him into your acount! But, surely, if you love or fear God yourself, this will be your first consideration,—In what business will your son be most likely to love and serve God? In what employment will he have the greatest advantage for laying up treasure in Heaven? I have been shocked above measure in observing how little this is attended to, even by pious parents! Even these consider only how he may get most money. . . . Even these send him to a heathen employer, and into a family where there is not the very form, much less the power, of religion. Upon this motive they fix him in a business which will necessarily expose him to such temptations as will leave him not a probability, if a possibility, of serving God.

FAMILY RELIGION

16

The person in your house that claims your first and nearest attention is, undoubtedly, your wife; seeing you are to love her, even as Christ hath loved the Church. . . .

Next to your wife are your children, immortal spirits whom God hath, for a time, entrusted to your care, that you may train them up in all holiness, and fit them for the enjoyment of God in eternity. This is a glorious and important trust; seeing one soul is of more value than all the world beside.

FAMILY RELIGION

17

I have been reflecting on my past life; I have been wandering up and down between fifty and sixty years, endeavouring in my poor way to do a little good to my fellow-creatures; and now it is probable that there are but a few steps between me and death; and what have I to trust to for salvation? I can see nothing which I have done or suffered that will bear looking at. I have no other plea than this:

I the chief of sinners am,
But Jesus died for me.

TO JOSEPH BRADFORD, 1783

18

From the time that power, riches and honour of all kinds were heaped upon the Christians, vice of all kinds came in like a flood, both on the clergy and laity. From the time that the Church and State, the kingdoms of Christ and of the world, were so strangely and unnaturally blended together, Christianity and heathenism were so thoroughly incorporated with each other, that they will hardly ever be divided till Christ comes to reign upon earth.

FORMER TIMES

19

Between twelve and one I preached at Freshford, and on White's Hill, near Bradford, in the evening. I had designed to preach there again the next evening, but a gentleman in the town desired me to preach at his door. The beasts of the people were tolerably quiet till I had nearly finished my sermon. They then lifted up their voice, especially one, called a gentleman, who had filled his pocket with rotten eggs. But a young man coming unawares, clapped his hands on each side and smashed them all at once. In an instant he was perfume all over, though it was not so sweet as balsam!

JOURNAL, 19th SEPTEMBER 1769

20

We see (and who does not?) the numberless follies and miseries of our fellow-creatures. We see on every side, either men of no religion at all, or men of a lifeless, formal religion. We are grieved at the sight; and should greatly rejoice if by any means we might convince some that there is a better religion to be attained—a religion worthy of God that gave it. And this we conceive to be no other than love; the love of God and of all mankind; the loving God with all our heart and soul and strength, as having first loved *us,* as the fountain of all the good we have received, and of all we ever hope to enjoy; and the loving every soul which God hath made, every man on earth, as our own soul.

AN EARNEST APPEAL

21

For several years, while my brother and I travelled on foot, our manner was for him that walked behind to read aloud some book of history, poetry or philosophy. Afterwards for many years (as my time at home was spent mostly in writing) it was my custom to read things of a lighter nature, chiefly when I was on horseback. Of late years, since a friend gave me a chaise, I have read them in my carriage. But it is not in this manner I treat the Scriptures: these I read and meditate upon day and night. It was not *in running* that I wrote twice over the *Notes on the New Testament* (to say nothing of those on the *Old*), containing above 800 quarto pages.

TO THE GAZETTEER, 1776

22

Before I conclude I beg leave, in my turn, to give you a few advices. 1. Be calm. Do not venture into the field again, till you are master of your temper. 2. Be good-natured. Passion is not commendable, but ill-nature even less. 3. Be courteous. Show good manners as well as good-nature to your opponent of whatever kind. 4. Be merciful. When you have gained an advantage over your opponent, do not press it to the uttermost. Remember the honest Quaker's advice: 'Art thou not content to lay John Wesley upon his back, but thou wilt tread his guts out?'

REMARKS ON MR HILL'S FARRAGO

23

When a man of huge possessions was boasting to his friend of the largeness of his estate, Socrates desired him to bring him a map of the earth, and to point out Attica therein. When this was done, he next desired Alcibiades to point out his own estate therein. When he could not do this, it was easy to observe how trifling his possessions were, in which he so prided himself, in comparison of the whole earth. . . . And what is the whole globe to the infinity of space!

THE ETERNITY OF GOOD

24

Has any man a right to use another as a slave?

Liberty is the right of every human creature as soon as he breathes the vital air. . . .

Give liberty to whom liberty is due, that is, to every child of man. Let none serve you but by his own act and deed, by his own voluntary choice. Away with all whips, all chains, all compulsion! Be gentle toward all men.

THOUGHTS ON SLAVERY

Justice is the life and soul of government, Without which it is no better than a dead carcase.

THE DUTIES OF HUSBANDS AND WIVES

25

We should never speak contemptuously of the Church, or anything pertaining to it. In some sense it is the mother of us all, who have been brought up therein. We ought never to make her blemishes matter of diversion, but rather of solemn sorrow before God.

REASONS AGAINST A SEPARATION FROM THE
CHURCH OF ENGLAND

The unworthiness of the minister doth not hinder the efficacy of God's ordinance. The reason is plain, because the efficacy is derived, not from him that administers but from him that ordains it. . . .

The word of God is not bound, though uttered by an unholy minister; and the Sacraments are not dry breasts, whether he that administers be holy or unholy.

ATTENDING THE CHURCH SERVICE

26

Never was there a time when it was more necessary for all that fear God, both in England and in America, to stir up the gift of God that is in them and wrestle with God in mighty prayer.

TO THOMAS RANKIN, 1775

I let you loose, George, on the great continent of America. Publish your message in the open face of the sun, and do all the good you can.

TO GEORGE SHADFORD, 1773

I have no prejudice to any man in America; I love you as my brethren and countrymen.

A CALM ADDRESS TO OUR AMERICAN COLONIES

27

The love of money, we know, is the root of all evil; but not the thing itself. The fault does not lie in the money, but in them that use it. It may be used ill; and what may not? But it may likewise be used well; it is full as applicable to the best as to the worst uses. It is of unspeakable service to all civilized nations in all the common affairs of life.

THE USE OF MONEY

Money never stays with me; it would burn if it did. I throw it out of my hands as soon as possible, lest it should find a way into my heart.

TO MRS HALL, 1768

Who can gain money without, in some measure, losing grace!

TO MARY BISHOP, 1777

28

Preach abroad . . . if ever you would do good. It is the cooping yourself up in rooms that has damped the work of God, which never was and never will be carried on to any purpose without going out into the highways and hedges and compelling poor sinners to come in . . . .

Preach abroad in every place. Mind not lazy or cowardly Methodists.

TO JAMES REA, 1766

It is a shame for any Methodist preacher to confine himself to one place. We are debtors to all the world.

TO JOSEPH BENSON, 1772

29

I am determined there shall be no circuits in England with more than four preachers as long as I live. Four are too many, if I can help it.

TO WM HORNER, 1790

I never was fond of multiplying circuits without an absolute necessity.

TO THOS HANSON, 1782

I do not advise you to go on too fast. It is not expedient to break up more ground than you can keep, to preach at any more places than you or your brethren can constantly attend. To preach once in a place and no more very seldom does any good.

TO FREEBORN GARRETTSON, 1786

30

By what right do you exclude women, any more than men, from choosing their own governors? Are they not free agents, as well as men? Have they not a will of their own? Are they not members of the State? Are they not part of the individuals that compose it? . . . By what argument do you prove that women are not naturally as free as men? . . .

By what right do you exclude a man from being one of the people, because he has not forty shillings a year, yea, or not a groat? Is he not a man whether he be rich or poor? Has he not a soul and a body? Has he not the nature of a man, consequently all the rights of a man, and all that flow from human nature; and, among the rest, that of not being controlled by any, but by his own consent?

OBSERVATIONS ON LIBERTY

OCTOBER

1

The love of liberty is the glory of rational beings; and it is the glory of Britons in particular.

. . . . .

Where is there a nation in Europe, in the habitable world, which enjoys such liberty of conscience as the English?

. . . . .

Neither you nor I can shew to any man in his senses that we have one chain upon us, even as big as a knitting-needle.

. . . . .

We enjoy at this day throughout these kingdoms such liberty, civil and religious, as no other kingdom or commonwealth in Europe or in the world, enjoys; and such as our ancestors never enjoyed from the Conquest to the Revolution.

THOUGHTS UPON LIBERTY

2

What is that liberty, properly so called, which every wise and good man desires? It is either religious or civil. Religious liberty is a liberty to choose our own religion, to worship God according to our own conscience, according to the best light we have. Every man living, as man, has a right to this, as he is a rational creature. And every man must judge for himself, because every man must give an account of himself to God. . . .

What is civil liberty? A liberty to enjoy our lives and fortunes in our own way; to use our property, whatever is legally our own, according to our own choice.

THOUGHTS UPON LIBERTY

3

If my argument has an odd appearance, yet let none think I am in jest. I am in great earnest. So have I need to be. For I am pleading the cause of my King, and Country, yea, of every country under heaven where there is any regular government. I am pleading against those principles that naturally tend to anarchy and confusion; that directly tend to unhinge all government, and overturn it from the foundation. But they are principles which are so encumbered with such difficulties as the wisest man living cannot remove.

.   .   .   .   .

The supposition that *the people* are the origin of power, or that 'all government is the creature of the people', though Mr Locke himself should attempt to defend it, is utterly indefensible.

OBSERVATIONS ON LIBERTY

4

Suppose a woman that loves God is addressed by an agreeable man, genteel, lively, entertaining, suitable in all other respects, though not religious; what should she do in such a case? What she *should* do, if she believes the Bible, is sufficiently clear. But what *can* she do? Is not this 'a test for human frailty too severe'? Who is able to stand in such a trial? Who can resist such a temptation! None but one that holds fast the shield of faith, and earnestly cries to the Strong for strength.

FRIENDSHIP WITH THE WORLD

5

In what manner do you transact your worldly business? I trust with diligence: whatever your hand findeth to do, doing it with all your might; in justice, rendering to all their due, in every circumstance of life; yea, and in mercy, doing unto every man what you would he should do unto you. This is well; but a Christian is called to go still farther, to add piety to justice; to intermix prayer, especially the prayer of the heart, with all the labour of his hands.

THE MORE EXCELLENT WAY

6

In a Christian believer *love* sits upon the throne, which is erected in the inmost soul, namely, love to God and man, which fills the whole heart and reigns without a rival. In a circle near the throne are all *holy tempers:* longsuffering, gentleness, meekness, fidelity, temperance. . . . In an exterior circle are all the *word of mercy,* whether to the souls or bodies of men. . . . Next to these are those that are usually termed *works of piety:* reading and hearing the Word, public, family and private prayer, receiving the Lord's Supper, fasting or abstinence. Lastly, that His followers may the more effectually provoke one another to love, holy tempers and good works, our Blessed Lord has united them together in one body, *the Church,* dispersed all over the earth, a little emblem of which, of the Church universal, we have in every particular Christian congregation.

ZEAL

7

We must build with one hand, while we fight with the other. And this is the great work, not only to bring souls to believe in Christ, but to build them up in our most holy faith.

MARY BISHOP, 1772

Redeem the time, catch the golden moments as they fly.

TO MRS JOHNSON, 1784

Your concern is with the present moment; your business is to live to-day.

TO A YOUNG DISCIPLE, 1771

8

Every Christian ought, undoubtedly, to be zealous for *the Church,* bearing a strong affection for it and earnestly desiring its prosperity and increase. He ought to be thus zealous, as for the Church universal, praying for it continually, so especially for that particular Church or Christian Society whereof he himself is a member. For this he ought to wrestle with God in prayer, meantime using every means in his power to enlarge its borders, and to strengthen his brethren.

.   .   .   .   .

But be most zealous of all for *love,* the queen of all graces, the highest perfection in earth or heaven, the very image of the invisible God, as in men below, so in angels above. For God is love, and he that dwelleth in love, dwelleth in God, and God in him.

ZEAL

9

You that are young have several advantages that are almost peculiar to yourselves. You have generally a flow of spirits and a liveliness of temper, which, by the grace of God, make you willing to undertake, and capable of performing many good works, at which others would be discouraged. And you have your health and strength of body, whereby you are eminently qualified to assist the sick and those that have no strength. You are able to take up and carry the crosses which may be expected to lie in the way. Employ then your whole vigour of body and mind in ministering to your afflicted brethren. And bless God that you have them to employ in so honourable a service.

VISITING THE SICK

10

See that you be courteous towards all men. It matters not, in this respect, whether they are high or low, rich or poor, superior or inferior to you. . . . The lowest and worst have a claim to our courtesy . . . Education cannot give courtesy of heart. . . . I have seen as real courtesy in an Irish cabin as could be found in St James's or the Louvre.

.   .   .   .   .

Labour to be of a calm, dispassionate temper.

.   .   .   .   .

You like to be honoured, but had you not rather be beloved.

PLEASING ALL MEN

11

Let love not visit you as a transient guest, but be the constant temper of your soul. See that your heart is filled at all times and on all occasions with real undissembled benevolence, not to those only that love you, but to every soul of man. Let it pant in your heart, let it sparkle in your eyes, let it shine in all your actions. Whenever you open your lips, let it be with love: and let there be on your tongue the law of kindness. . . . Be not straitened or limited in your affection, but let it embrace every child of man. Every one that is born of a woman has a claim to your good-will. . . . Be as eyes to the blind, as feet to the lame; a husband to the widow, and a father to the fatherless.

PLEASING ALL MEN

12

I borrowed here a volume of Lord Chesterfield's *Letters* which I had heard very highly commended. And what did I learn? That he was a man of much wit, middling sense and some learning; but as absolutely void of virtue as any heathen that ever lived. I say not only void of all religion (for I doubt whether he believed there is a God), but even of virtue, of justice and mercy, which he never once recommended to his son. And truth he sets at open defiance; he continually guards him against it; half his letters inculcate deep dissimulation as the most necessary of all accomplishments. Add to this, his studiously instilling into the young man all the principles of debauchery, when himself was between seventy and eighty years old. . . . And this is the favourite of the age!

JOURNAL 12th OCTOBER 1775

13

Question: What is a sufficient call to a new place?

Answer. 1. An invitation from a serious man, fearing God, who has a house to receive us. 2. A probability of doing more good by going thither than by staying longer where we are.

MINUTES OF CONVERSATIONS, 1744

That is a doubt with me too whether you do right in preaching to twelve or fifteen persons. I fear it is making the Gospel too cheap, and will not therefore blame any assistant for removing the meeting from any place where the congregation does not usually amount to twenty persons.

TO EDWARD JACKSON, 1781

14

Upon cool and impartial consideration, it will appear that the former days were not better than these. . . . While luxury and profaneness have been increasing on the one hand, on the other, benevolence and compassion toward all forms of human woe have increased in a manner not known before, from the earliest ages. In proof of this, we see more hospitals, infirmaries and other places of public charity. . . . We have cause to bless God.

FORMER TIMES

15

It has been loudly affirmed that most of those persons now in connexion with me, who believe it their duty to call sinners to repentance, having been taken immediately from low trades, tailors, shoemakers, and the like, are a set of poor, stupid, illiterate men, that scarcely know their right hand from their left; yet I cannot but say that I would sooner cut off my right hand than suffer one of them to speak a word in any of our Chapels, if I had not reasonable proof that he had more knowledge in the Holy Scriptures, more knowledge of himself, more knowledge of God and the things of God, than nine in ten of the clergymen I have conversed with, either at the Universities or elsewhere.

ATTENDING THE CHURCH SERVICE

16

As our bodies are strengthened by bread and wine, so are our souls by these tokens of the Body and the Blood of Christ. This is the food of our souls; this gives strength to perform our duty, and leads us on to perfection. If therefore we have any regard for the plain command of Christ, if we desire the pardon of our sins, if we wish for strength to believe, to love and obey God, then we should neglect no opportunity of receiving the Lord's Supper.

If we consider the Lord's Supper as a command of Christ, no man can have any pretence to Christian piety, who does not receive it, not once a month, but as often as he can.

THE DUTY OF CONSTANT COMMUNION

17

Whatever God commands us to do, we are to do, because he commands, whether we feel any benefit thereby or not. Now God commands: 'This do in remembrance of Me.' This, therefore, we are to do because he commands, whether we find present benefit thereby or not. But undoubtedly we shall find benefit sooner or later, though perhaps insensibly. We shall be insensibly strengthened, made more fit for the service of God, and more constant in it.

THE DUTY OF CONSTANT COMMUNION

18

A second reason why every Christian should do this as often as he can, is because the benefits of doing it are so great to all that do it in faith and in obedience to him; viz. the forgiveness of our past sins, the present strengthening and refreshing of our souls. In this world we are never free from temptations. Whatever way of life we are in, whatever our conditions be, whether we are sick or well, in trouble or at ease, the enemies of our souls are watching to lead us into sin. And too often they prevail over us. Now, when we are convinced of having sinned against God, what surer way have we of procuring pardon from him than the showing forth the Lord's death; and beseeching him, for the sake of his Son's sufferings, to blot out all our sins?

THE DUTY OF CONSTANT COMMUNION

19

The Methodists grow more and more self-indulgent because they grow rich. Although many of them are still deplorably poor, yet many others, in the space of twenty, thirty or forty years, are twenty, thirty, yea, a hundred times richer than they were when they first entered the Society. And it is an observation which admits of few exceptions, that nine in ten of these, decreased in grace, in the same proportion as they increased in wealth.

·   ·   ·   ·   ·

I call God to record upon my soul, that I advise no man more than I practise. I do, blessed be God, gain and save and give all I can. And so, I trust in God, I shall do, while the breath of God is in my nostrils.

CAUSES OF THE INEFFICACY OF CHRISTIANITY

20

Hold up a stone in the air; the moment you withdraw your hand it naturally falls to the ground. In like manner, were he to withdraw his hand for a moment, the creation would fall into nothing.

SPIRITUAL WORSHIP

You cannot possibly suppose the sun or skies to be God, any more than you can suppose a god of wood or stone. And, further, whoever believes all things to be mere matter must of course believe that all things are governed by dire necessity. Necessity that is as inexorable as the winds, as ruthless as the rocks, as merciless as the waves that dash upon them!

FAITH

21

Does it not seem (and yet this cannot be) that Christianity, true, scriptural Christianity, has a tendency, in process of time, to undermine amd destroy itself? For wherever true Christianity spreads, it must cause diligence and frugality, which, in the natural course of things, must beget riches. And riches beget pride, love of the world, and every temper that is destructive of Christianity. Now if there be no way to prevent this, then Christianity is inconsistent with itself, and of consequence cannot stand, cannot continue long among any people, since wherever it generally prevails, it saps its own foundation.

CAUSES OF THE INEFFICACY OF CHRISTIANITY

Prefer grace before gold and precious stones; glory in heaven to riches on earth.

A SINGLE EYE

22

Christianity, considered as an inward principle, is holiness and happiness, the image of God impressed on a created spirit; a fountain of peace and love springing up into everlasting life. And this I conceive to be the strongest evidence of the truth of Christianity. I do not undervalue traditional evidence. Let it have its place and its due honour. It is highly serviceable in its kind, and in its degree. And yet I cannot set it on a level with this.

TO DR MIDDLETON, 1748-9

23

A Christian is full of love to his neighbour, of universal love; not confined to one sect or party; not restrained to those who agree with him in opinions, in outward modes of worship; or to those who are allied to him by blood or recommended by nearness of place. Neither does he love those only that love him or are endeared to him by intimacy of acquaintance. But his love resembles that of Him, whose mercy is over all his works. It soars above all these scanty bounds, embracing neighbours and strangers, friends and enemies.

TO DR MIDDLETON, 1748-9

24

It is a fundamental principle with us that to renounce reason is to renounce religion, that religion and reason go hand in hand and that all irrational religion is false religion. . . . I caution my followers against judging of the spirit by which any one speaks by their own inward feelings; because these, being of a doubtful nature, may come from God, or may not.

TO DR RUTHERFORTH, 1768

I have often found an aptness both in myself and others to connect events that have no real relation to each other. So one says: 'I am as sure this is the will of God as that I am justified.' Another says: 'God as surely spake this to my heart as ever he spoke to me at all.' This is an exceedingly dangerous way of thinking or speaking.

TO ANN BOLTON, 1785

25

For several years I was moderator in the disputations which were held six times a week at Lincoln College in Oxford. I could not avoid acquiring thereby some degree of expertness in arguing, and especially in discerning and pointing out well-covered and plausible fallacies. I have since found abundant reason to praise God, for giving me this honest art.

.   .   .   .   .

Shifting, subtlety and disguise, I despise and abhor.

.   .   .   .   .

All my designs and thought and care and labour were directed to this one point, to advance the Kingdom of Christ on earth.

REMARKS ON DR ERSKINE'S DEFENCE

26

You mistake one thing. It is I, not the Conference, that station the preachers; but I do it at the time of Conference that I may have the advice of my brethren. But I have no thought of removing you from the Glamorganshire Circuit; you are just in your right place. But you say: 'Many of the people are asleep.' They are; and you are sent to awake them out of sleep. 'But they are dead.' True; and you are sent to raise the dead. But you have need to be all alive yourselves if you would impart life to others.

TO ZACHARIAH YEWDALL, 1780

27

Whoever has the necessities and conveniences of life for himself and his family, and a little to spare for them that have not, is properly a rich man.

.   .   .   .   .

Beware of forming a hasty judgment concerning the fortune of others.

.   .   .   .   .

By whatsoever means thy riches increase, whether with or without labour, whether by trade, legacies, or any other way, unless thy charities increase in the same proportion, unless thou givest a full tenth of thy substance, of thy fixed and occasional income, thou dost undoubtedly set thy heart upon thy gold, and it shall eat thy flesh as fire.

THE DANGER OF INCREASING RICHES

28

Much money does not imply much sense; neither does a good estate infer a good understanding. As a gay coat may cover a bad heart, so a fair peruke may adorn a weak head.

.   .   .   .   .

Men are unhappy because they are unholy. Pain accompanies and follows sin. Why is the earth so full of complicated distress? Because it is full of complicated wickedness.

It is impossible, in the nature of things, that wickedness can consist with happiness.

DOCTRINE OF ORIGINAL SIN

How many take holiness and harmlessness to mean one and the same thing? Whereas, were a man as harmless as a post, he might be as far from holiness, as heaven from earth.

THE WEDDING GARMENT

29

It is hardly credible of how great consequence before God the smallest things are; and what great inconveniences sometimes follow those which appear to be light faults.

As a very little dust will disorder a clock, and the least grain of sand will obscure our sight, so the least grain of sin which is upon the heart will hinder its right motion towards God. . . .

As the most dangerous winds may enter at little openings, so the devil never enters more dangerously than by little unobserved incidents, which seem to be nothing, yet insensibly open the heart to great temptations.

A PLAIN ACCOUNT OF CHRISTIAN PERFECTION

30

Have a pure intention of heart, a steadfast regard to His glory in all your actions.

.   .   .   .   .

Many mistakes may consist with pure love. Some may accidentally flow from it. I mean, love itself may incline us to mistake.

.   .   .   .   .

To imagine none can teach you but those who are themselves saved from sin, is a very great and dangerous mistake. Give no place to it for a moment.

A PLAIN ACCOUNT OF CHRISTIAN PERFECTION

31

There is in the heart of every child of man an inexhaustible fund of ungodliness and unrighteousness, deeply and strongly rooted in the soul, that nothing less than Almighty Grace can cure it.

THE DECEITFULNESS OF MAN'S HEART

Men are generally lost in the hurry of life, in the business or pleasures of it, and seem to think that their regeneration, their new nature, will spring and grow up within them, with as little care and thought of their own, as their bodies were conceived and have attained their full strength and stature.

GRIEVING THE HOLY SPIRIT

NOVEMBER

1

A man of a truly Catholic spirit is fixed in his congregation as well as in his principles. . . . But while he is steadily fixed in his religious principles, in what he believes to be the truth as it is in Jesus; while he firmly adheres to that worship of God which he judges to be most acceptable in his sight, and while he is united by the tenderest and closest ties to one particular congregation, his heart is enlarged toward all mankind, those he knows and those he knows not; he embraces with strong and cordial affection neighbours and strangers, friends and enemies. This is Catholic or universal love. And he that has this is of a Catholic spirit.

A CATHOLIC SPIRIT

2

No man can choose for, or prescribe to another. But every one must follow the dictates of his own conscience, in simplicity and godly sincerity. He must be fully persuaded in his own mind, and then act according to the best light he has. Nor has any creature power to constrain another to walk by his own rule. God has given no right to any of the children of men thus to lord it over the consciences of his brethren. But every man must judge for himself.

.   .   .   .   .

I dare not presume to impose my mode of worship on any other. I believe it is truly primitive and apostolical. But my belief is no rule for another.

A CATHOLIC SPIRIT

3

Though we cannot think alike, may we not love alike?

.   .   .   .   .

Every wise man will allow others the same liberty of thinking which he desires they should allow him, and will no more insist on their embracing his opinions, than he would have them to insist on his embracing theirs.

A CATHOLIC SPIRIT

4

God can give the end without any means at all; but you have no reason to think he will. Therefore constantly and carefully use all the means which he has appointed to be the ordinary channels of his grace.

THE NATURE OF ENTHUSIASM

Encourage whomsoever God is pleased to employ. . . . Speak well of him wheresoever you are; defend his character and his mission. Enlarge, as far as you can, his sphere of action. Shew him all kindness in word and deed. And cease not to cry to God on his behalf, that he may save both himself and them that hear him.

CAUTION AGAINST BIGOTRY

5

So far as in conscience thou canst (retaining still thy own opinions, and thy own manner of worshipping God), join with me in the work of God, and let us go on hand in hand.

.   .   .   .   .

A man of a true Catholic spirit is fixed as the sun, in his judgment concerning the main branches of Christian doctrine. It is true, he is always ready to hear and weigh whatsoever can be offered against his principles. But as this does not shew any wavering in his own mind, so neither does it occasion any. He does not halt between two opinions, nor vainly endeavour to blend them into one.

A CATHOLIC SPIRIT

6

We must act as each is fully persuaded in his own mind. Hold you fast that which you believe is most acceptable to God, and I will do the same. I believe the episcopal form of Church government to be scriptural and apostolical. If you think the Presbyterian or Independent is better, think so still and act accordingly. I believe infants ought to be baptized, and that this may be done either by dipping or sprinkling. If you are otherwise persuaded, be so still, and follow your own persuasion. It appears to me that forms of prayer are of excellent use, particularly in the great congregation. If you judge extemporary prayer to be of more use, act suitable to your own judgment. . . . If thou love God and all mankind, I ask no more. 'Give me thine hand.'

A CATHOLIC SPIRIT

7

Keep you your opinion; I mine and that as steadily as ever. You need not endeavour to come over to me or bring me over to you. I do not desire you to dispute these points, or to hear or speak one word concerning them. Let all opinions alone on one side and the other. Only 'give me thine hand.'

·   ·   ·   ·   ·

Speak honourably, wherever thou art, of the work of God, by whomsoever he works, and kindly of his messengers. And if it be in thy power, not only sympathize with them when they are in any difficulty or distress, but give them a cheerful and effectual assistance.

A CATHOLIC SPIRIT

8

To be singular, merely for singularity's sake, is not the part of a Christian.

·   ·   ·   ·   ·

Let all your apparel be as clean as your situation in life will allow.

ADVICE WITH REGARD TO DRESS

What is more insufferable to a man in a passion, than to see you keep your temper?

FREE THOUGHTS ON PUBLIC AFFAIRS, 1788

9

Having procured an apparatus on purpose, I ordered several persons to be electrified, who were ill of various disorders; some of whom found an immediate, some a gradual, cure. From this time I appointed, first some hours in every week, and afterward an hour in every day, wherein any that desired it might try the virtue of this surprising medicine. Two or three years after, our patients were so numerous that we were obliged to divide them. So part were electrified in Southwark, part at the Foundery, others near St Paul's, and the rest near the Seven Dials. The same method we have taken ever since; and to this day, while hundreds perhaps thousands, have received unspeakable good, I have not known one man, woman or child who has received any hurt thereby.

JOURNAL, 9th NOVEMBER 1756

10

The greater the share *the people* have in the government, the less liberty, either civil or religious, does the nation in general enjoy. Accordingly, there is most liberty of all, civil and religious, under a limited monarchy; there is usually less under an aristocracy; and least of all under a democracy.

OBSERVATIONS ON LIBERTY

I do not defend the measures which have been taken with regard to America; I doubt whether any man can defend them, either on the foot of law, equity or prudence.

FREE THOUGHTS ON PUBLIC AFFAIRS, 1788

11

In the year 1729 I met with Kempis' *Christian Pattern*. The nature and extent of inward religion, the religion of the heart, now appeared to me in a stronger light than ever it had done before. I saw that giving even all my life to God (supposing it possible to do this, and go no further) would profit me nothing, unless I gave my heart. . . .

A year or two after, Mr Law's *Christian Perfection* and *Serious Call* were put into my hands. These convinced me more than ever of the absolute impossibility of being half a Christian.

In the year 1729 I began not only to read but to study the Bible, as the one and only standard of truth and the only model of pure religion.

A PLAIN ACCOUNT OF CHRISTIAN PERFECTION

12

Obey and regard them that are over you in the Lord, and do not think you know better than they. . . .

If you have at any time thought, spoke or acted wrong, be not backward to acknowledge it. . . .

Be open and frank when you are taxed with any thing; do not seek to evade or disguise it.

.   .   .   .   .

Beware of judging people to be either right or wrong, by your own feelings.

A PLAIN ACCOUNT OF CHISTIAN PERFECTION

13

Do not hastily ascribe things to God. Do not easily suppose dreams, voices, impressions, visions or revelations to be from

God. They may be from him. They may be from nature. They may be from the devil.

.   .   .   .   .

I advise you never to use the words *wisdom, reason,* or *knowledge,* by way of reproach. On the contrary, pray that you yourself may abound in them more and more.

.   .   .   .   .

I entreat you, beware of bigotry. Let not your love or benevolence be confined to Methodists.

A PLAIN ACCOUNT OF CHRISTIAN PERFECTION

14

Do all the good you possibly can do to the bodies and souls of men. . . .
Be *active.* Give no place to indolence or sloth. . . .
Be always employed; lose no shred of time; gather up the fragments, that none be lost.

.   .   .   .   .

Do not talk much; neither long at a time. Few can converse properly for above an hour. Keep at the utmost distance from pious chit-chat, from religious gossiping.

A PLAIN ACCOUNT OF CHRISTIAN PERFECTION

15

Beware of schism, of making a rent in the Church of Christ. . . .
Beware of a dividing spirit.

.   .   .   .   .

Do not run down any preacher.

.   .   .   .   .

Beware of impatience of contradiction. Do not condemn or think hardly of those who cannot see just as you see, or who judge it their duty to contradict you.

A PLAIN ACCOUNT OF CHRISTIAN PERFECTION

16

Beware of touchiness or testiness; not bearing to be spoken to; starting at the least word. . . .

Expect contradictions and opposition, together with crosses of various kinds.

.   .   .   .   .

Give no offence which can possibly be avoided.

.   .   .   .   .

We are to bear with those we cannot amend.

A PLAIN ACCOUNT OF CHRISTIAN PERFECTION

17

The sea is an excellent figure of the fulness of God, and that of the blessed Spirit. For as the rivers all return to the sea, so the bodies, the souls, and the good works of the righteous, return to God.

.   .   .   .   .

The bottom of the soul may be in repose, even while we are in many outward troubles; just as the bottom of the sea is calm, while the surface is strongly agitated.

A PLAIN ACCOUNT OF CHRISTIAN PERFECTION

As thinking is the act of an embodied spirit, playing upon a set of material keys, it is not strange that the soul can make but ill music when her instrument is out of tune.

TO MRS BENNIS, 1771

18

To abandon all, to strip oneself of all, in order to seek and follow Jesus Christ, naked to Bethlehem, where he was born, naked to the hall, where he was scourged; and naked to Calvary, where he died on the Cross, is so great a mercy, that neither the thing nor the knowledge of it is given to any but through faith in the Son of God.

Of the sins which God has pardoned, let nothing remain but a deeper humility in the heart. . . .

There is no love of God without patience, and no patience without lowliness and sweetness of spirit.

A PLAIN ACCOUNT OF CHRISTIAN PERFECTON

19

One of the principle rules of religion is to lose no occasion of serving God. And since he is invisible to our eyes, we are to serve him in our neighbour, which he receives as if done to himself in person, standing visibly before us. . . .

Good works do not receive their last perfection till they, as it were, lose themselves in God. . . .

Absolute perfection belongs not to men nor to angels, but to God alone.

A PLAIN ACCOUNT OF CHRISTIAN PERFECTION

20

On every occasion of uneasiness we should retire to prayer, that we may give place to the grace and light of God. . . .

Prayer continues in the desire of the heart, though the understanding is employed on outward things.

A PLAIN ACCOUNT OF CHRISTIAN PERFECTION

Hypocrisy or insincerity is the first thing to guard against in prayer. Beware not to speak what thou dost not mean.

SERMON ON THE MOUNT, VI

21

I will not, I dare not draw the saw of controversy any longer; especially with James Deaves, who will dispute through a stone wall.

In the name of God, have done! You can do no good by disputing. But you do much harm. You hurt your own spirit. You hurt others. You blow up a flame. You damp and hinder the work of God. By tale bearing you separate chief friends. You prejudice my intimate friends against *me*. I have not deserved it of you. Let me alone. I act according to the best of my judgment.

TO ARTHUR KEENE, 1789

22

There is a poor, queer old woman in Bristol (if she is not gone to Paradise) with whom it might do you good to talk. John Jones knows her. Her name is Elizabeth Edgecomb.

TO DOROTHY FURLY, 1757

I hope you have talked with Cornelius Bastable, as well as heard him preach. He is an uncommon monument of the power of grace, strengthening the understanding, as well as renewing the heart. For so weak a head and so bad a temper as he once had, I do not know anything among all our preachers.

TO DOROTHY FURLY, 1759

23

If you can persuade honest Alice Brammah to be cleanly as well as gentle, she will be tenfold more useful; and so will Billy Brammah, if he will be teachable and advisable.

TO DOROTHY FURLY, 1776

Sister Snowden is good-natured, but is a consummate slut; explain with her largely on this head; convince her that it is both a sin and a shame. She came into a clean house at Stroud; let her take care to keep it clean for the honour of God—for the honour of her husband—for the honour of her country.

TO WILLIAM SEVERN, 1776

24

Faith is that divine evidence whereby the spiritual man discerneth God and the things of God. It is with regard to the spiritual world what sense is with regard to the natural. It is the spiritual sensation of every soul that is born of God. . . . Faith is the eye of the new-born soul. . . .

By this faith we are saved from all uneasiness of mind, from the anguish of a wounded spirit, from discontent, from fear and sorrow of heart, and from that inexpressible listlessness and weariness, both of the world and of ourselves, which we had so helplessly laboured under for many years. . . . In this we find that love of God, and of all mankind, which we had elsewhere sought in vain. This we know and feel and therefore cannot but declare, saves every one that partakes of it, from sin and misery, from every unhappy and unholy temper.

AN EARNEST APPEAL

25

Whenever you see an unreasonable man, you see one who perhaps calls himself a Christian, but is no more a Christian than he is an angel. So far as he departs from true, genuine reason, so far he departs from Christianity. . . .

The lives of those who are *called* Christians is no just objection to Christianity. We join with you in desiring a religion founded on reason, and every way agreeable thereto. . . .

We not only allow, but earnestly exhort all who seek after true religion, to use all the reason which God hath given them, in searching out the things of God.

AN EARNEST APPEAL

26

Every man has authority to save the life of a dying man.

.   .   .   .   .

He is no physician who works no cure.

.   .   .   .   .

Every Christian, if he is able to do it, has authority to save a dying soul.

He that saves no souls is no minister of Christ.

TO A CLERGYMAN, 1748

I may bring many others to the kingdom of Heaven, and yet myself never enter there.

SERMON ON THE MOUNT, XIII

27

I wish he[1] would see Dr Whitehead. I am persuaded there is not such another physician in England; although (to confound human wisdom) he does not know how to cure his own wife.

TO HIS NIECE, SARAH WESLEY, 1788

I think Mr Woodhouse will not die yet, unless it be by the help of physicians and surgeons.

TO MRS WOODHOUSE, 1775

Seeing life and health are things of so great importance, it is without question, highly expedient that physicians should have all possible advantages of learning and education.

TO A CLERGYMAN, 1748

28

I am sick of opinions. I am weary to bear them. My soul loathes this frothy food. Give me solid and substantial religion. Give me a humble, gentle lover of God and man, a man full of mercy and good fruits, without partiality and without hypocrisy, a man laying himself out in the work of faith, the patience of hope, the labour of love. Let my soul be with these Christians, wheresoever they are, and whatsoever opinion they are of.

A FARTHER APPEAL

[1]Charles Wesley.

29

The mariner may have many concerns to mind, and many businesses to engage his thoughts; but not when the ship is sinking.

.   .   .   .   .

All your stores will not save the sinking ship, unless you can stop the *leak*. Unless you can some way keep out these floods of ungodliness that are still continually pouring in, you must soon be swallowed up in the great deep, in the Abyss of God's judgments. This is the destruction of the English nation. It is vice bursting in on every side.

A FARTHER APPEAL

30

It is indeed a very great thing to speak in the name of God; it might make him that is of the stoutest heart tremble, if he considered that every time he speaks to others, his own soul is at stake.

.   .   .   .   .

I desire your words may be always the picture of your heart.

A FARTHER APPEAL

Give me one hundred preachers who fear nothing but sin and desire nothing but God, and I care not a straw whether they be clergymen or laymen, such alone will shake the gates of hell and set up the kingdom of Heaven on earth.

TO ALEXANDER MATHER, 1777

DECEMBER

1

One was asking me, several years since: 'What, are you one of the knight-errants? How, I pray, got Quixotism into your head? You want nothing; you have a good provision for life; and are in a way of preferment; and must you leave all, to fight windmills, to convert savages in America?' I could only reply: 'Sir, if the Bible is a lie, I am as very a madman as you can conceive. But if it be true, I am in my senses. I am neither madman nor Enthusiast.'

· · · · ·

Whenever it has pleased God to work any great work upon the earth, he hath stepped more or less out of the common way.

A FARTHER APPEAL

2

By salvation I mean, not barely, according to the vulgar notion, deliverance from hell or going to heaven, but a present deliverance from sin; a restoration of the soul to its primitive health, its original purity; a recovery of the divine nature; the renewal of our souls after the image of God.

· · · · ·

True religion is the loving God with all our heart, and our neighbour as ourselves; and in that love abstaining from all evil and doing all possible good to all men.

A FARTHER APPEAL

3

Religion is the spirit of a sound mind.

. . . . .

God has given us our own reason for a guide; though never excluding the secret assistance of his Spirit.

. . . . .

Trust not in visions or dreams; in sudden impressions or strong impulses of any kind. Remember, it is not by these you are to know what is the will of God on any particular occasion, but by applying the plain Scripture, with the help of experience and reason, and the ordinary assistance of the Spirit of God.

THE NATURE OF ENTHUSIASM

4

Ye do not walk in a vain shadow; God and eternity are real things.

SERMON ON THE MOUNT, I

Be a good steward of every gift of God, even of his lowest gifts.

SERMON ON THE MOUNT, IV

It is His love which gives a relish to all we taste, puts life and sweetness into all, while every creature leads us up to the great Creator, and all earth is a scale to heaven.

SERMON ON THE MOUNT, VIII

Enjoy whatever brings glory to God, and promotes peace and goodwill among men.

SERMON ON THE MOUNT, XIII

5

No wicked man is happy. The reason is plain. All unholy tempers are uneasy tempers.

THE NEW BIRTH

The more we grow in grace, the more do we see of the desperate wickedness of our heart.

SERMON ON THE MOUNT, I

The pure in heart see all things full of God.

SERMON ON THE MOUNT, III

6

It is certain none can be a good divine who is not a good textuary. . . .

There is yet another branch of knowledge highly necessary for a clergyman, and that is *knowledge of the world*; a knowledge of men, of their maxims, tempers and manners, such as they occur in real life. Without this he will be liable to receive much hurt, and capable of doing little good, as he will not know either how to deal with men according to the vast variety of their characters or to preserve himself from those who in almost every place lie in wait to deceive. . . .

Next to prudence or common sense, a clergyman ought certainly to have some degree of *good breeding;* I mean, address, easiness and propriety of behaviour, wherever his lot is cast.

Perhaps one might add, he should have all the courtesy of a gentleman joined with the correctness of a scholar.

ADDRESS TO THE CLERGY

7

You want lively, zealous, active preachers. And, to tell you a melancholy truth, few of our elder preachers are of this character. You must look for zeal and activity among the young preachers. I am greatly scandalized at this, that a preacher fifty years old is commonly but half a preacher.

TO ARTHUR KEENE, 1784

Is it not highly expedient that a guide of souls should have likewise some liveliness and readiness of thought? Or how will he be able, when need requires, to answer a fool according to his folly?

ADDRESS TO THE CLERGY

8

An ancient historian relates that when the Apostle was so enfeebled by age as not to be able to preach, he was frequently brought into the congregation in his chair, and just uttered: 'Beloved children, love one another.'

SPIRITUAL IDOLATRY

This love we believe to be the medicine of life, the never-failing remedy for all the evils of a disordered world, for all the miseries and vices of men. Wherever this is, there are virtue and happiness going hand in hand. 'Eternal sunshine of the spotless mind.'

AN EARNEST APPEAL

9

I went down at half past five, but found no preacher in the Chapel, though we had three or four in the house. So I preached myself. Afterwards, enquiring why none of my family attended the morning preaching, they said it was because they sat up so late. I resolved to put a stop to this; and therefore ordered that, 1. Every one under my roof should go to bed at nine, that, 2. Every one might attend the morning preaching. And so they have done, ever since.

JOURNAL, 9th DECEMBER 1787

10

I have not one hour to spare from four in the morning till nine at night.

.   .   .   .   .

You certainly need not want anything as long as I live.

TO CHARLES WESLEY, 1788

You see further into men than I do.

.   .   .   .   .

My letters to-day cost me eighteen shillings.

TO CHARES WESLEY, 1785

No man is a good judge in his own cause.

TO CHARLES WESLEY, 1775

11

To retain the grace of God is much more than to gain it; hardly one in three does this.

TO DR ADAM CLARKE, 1790

I wonder how any that have lost the love of God can find any rest in their souls till they have regained it.

TO MARTHA CHAPMAN, 1784

As you hear the wind, and feel it too, while it strikes upon your bodily organs, you will know you are under the guidance of God's Spirit the same way, namely, by feeling it in your soul; by the present peace, joy and love which you feel within, as well as by its outward and more distant effects.

JOURNAL, 31st JULY 1739

12

Are you persuaded you see more clearly than me? It is not unlikely that you may. Then treat me as you would desire to be treated yourself upon a change of circumstances. Point me out a better way than I have yet known. Show me it is so, by plain proof of Scripture. And if I linger in the path I have been accustomed to tread, and am therefore unwilling to leave it, labour with me a little; take me by the hand, and lead me as I am able to bear. But be not displeased if I entreat you not to beat me down in order to quicken my pace. I can go but feebly and slowly at best; then, I should not be able to go at all. May I not request of you, further, not to give me hard names in order to bring me into the right way? Suppose I were ever so much in the wrong, I doubt this would not set me right. Rather, it would make me run so much the farther from you, and so get more and more out of the way.

PREFACE TO SERMONS, 1747

13

I desire plain truth for plain people. Therefore of set purpose, I abstain from all nice and philosophical speculations; from all perplexed and intricate reasonings; and, as far as possible, from even the show of learning, unless in sometimes citing the original Scripture. I labour to avoid all words which are not easy to be understood, all which are not used in common life; and, in particular, those kinds of technical terms that so frequently occur in Bodies of Divinity; those modes of speaking which men of reading are intimately acquainted with, but which to common people are an unknown tongue. Yet I am not assured that I do not sometimes slide into them unawares. It is so extremely natural to imagine that a word which is familiar to ourselves is so to all the world.

PREFACE TO SERMONS, 1747

14

Is there need to apologize to sensible persons for the plainness of my style? . . . I dare no more write in a fine style than wear a fine coat. But were it otherwise, had I time to spare, I should still write just as I do. I should purposely decline what many admire, a highly-ornamented style. I cannot admire French oratory; I despise it from my heart. . . . Let who will admire the French frippery; I am still for plain sound English.

God himself has told us how to speak, both as to the matter and the manner . . . Let him aim at no more ornament than he finds in that sentence, which is the sum of the whole Gospel: 'We love him because he hath first loved us.'

PREPACE TO SERMONS, 1788

15

I am a creature of a day, passing through life as an arrow through the air. I am a spirit come from God and returning to God; just hovering over the great gulf, till, a few moments hence, I am no more seen; I drop into an unchangeable eternity. I want to know one thing—the way to heaven; how to land safe on that happy shore. God himself has condescended to teach the way; for this very end he came from heaven. He hath written it down in a book. O give me that book! At any price, give me the book of God! I have it; here is knowledge enough for me. Let me be *homo unius libri.*[1]

PREFACE TO SERMONS, 1774

16

My Lord,—I am a dying man, having already one foot in the grave. Humanly speaking, I cannot long creep upon the earth, being now nearer ninety than eighty years of age. But I cannot die in peace before I have discharged this office of Christian love to your Lordship. I write without ceremony, as neither hoping nor tearing anything from your Lordship or from any man living. . . . Does your Lordship know what the Methodists are? That many thousands of them are zealous members of the Church of England, and strongly attached not only to His Majesty, but to his present Ministry? Why should your Lordship, setting religion out of the question, throw away such a body of respectable friends? . . . Is this a time to persecute any man for conscience' sake? I beseech you, my Lord, do as you would be done to. You are a man of sense; you are a man of learning; nay, I verily believe (what is of infinitely more value), you are a man of piety. Then think, and let think. I pray God to bless you with the choicest of his blessings.

TO DR TOMLINE, BISHOP OF LINCOLN, 1790

[1] A man of one book.

17

Those that desire to write or say anything to me have no time to lose; for time has shaken me by the hand and death is not far behind. But I have reason to be thankful for the time that is past: I felt few of the infirmities of old age for fourscore and six years. It was not till a year and a half ago that my strength and my sight failed. And still I am enabled to scrawl a little and to creep, though I cannot run. Probably I should not be able to do so much did not many of you assist me by your prayers. . . . See that you never give place to one thought of separating from your brethren in Europe. Lose no opportunity of declaring to all men that the Methodists are one people in all the world.

TO EZEKIEL COOPER, 1791[1]

18

I really think it would be the most Christian and the most prudent way to conclude this matter amicably. I should advise you not to force the course of the river. . . . Shake off the dust of your feet against them, and go where you are welcome. . . . Law is the last and the worst means, though it is sometimes necessary. But I should expect far more from prayer.

TO DR ADAM CLARKE, 1787

Let us have no law if it be possible to avoid it: that is the last and worst remedy. Try every other remedy first.

TO SAMUEL BARDSLEY, 1789

[1]Wesley's last letter to America.

19

I am called to a peculiar work. And perhaps the very temper and behaviour which you blame is one great means whereby I am capacitated for carrying on that work. I do not lessen my authority over two hundred preachers and twenty thousand men and women by any tenderness either of speech or of behaviour, whether to preachers or people. God exceedingly confirms my authority thereby.

TO MRS CROSBY, 1763

The power I have, I never sought. It was the undesired, unexpected result of the work God was pleased to work by me. I have a thousand times sought to devolve it on others; but as yet I cannot. I therefore suffer it till I can find any to ease me of my burden.

TO THE REV. H. VENN, 1763

20

If you understand your particular calling as you ought, you will have no time that hangs upon your hands.

.   .   .   .   .

Never leave anything till to-morrow, which you can do to-day. And do it as well as possible. Do not sleep or yawn over it. Put your whole strength to the work. Spare no pains. Let nothing be done by halves or in a slight and careless manner.

.   .   .   .   .

We cannot study to ruin our neighbour's trade, in order to advance our own.

THE USE OF MONEY

21

Do not seek to be honourable; be content to be despised.

TO WM HORNER, 1790

Good breeding I love; but how difficult is it to keep it clear of affectation and of a something which does not well agree with that mind which was in Christ!

TO MARY BISHOP, 1781

I am become, I know not how, an honourable man. The scandal of the Cross is ceased; and all the kingdom, rich and poor, Papists and Protestants, behave with courtesy—nay, and seeming goodwill! It seems as if I had wellnigh finished my course, and our Lord was giving me an honourable discharge.

TO ELIZABETH RITCHIE, 1785

22

Gain all you can, by common sense, by using in your business all the understanding which God has given you.

.   .   .   .   .

You should be continually learning, from the experience of others or from your own experience, reading and reflection, to do everything you have to do, better to-day than you did yesterday. And see that you practise whatever you learn, that you may make the best of all that is in your hands.

THE USE OF MONEY

It is not always a defect to mind one thing at a time. And an aptness so to do, to employ the whole vigour of the mind on the thing in hand, may answer excellent purposes. Only you here need to be exceeding wary, lest the thing you pursue be wrong.

First, be well assured not only that it is good but that it is the best thing for you at that time; and then, whatsoever your hand findeth to do, do it with your might.

TO PHILOTHEA BRIGGS, 1772

23

Having gained all you can, by honest wisdom and unwearied diligence, the second rule of Christian prudence is: save all you can. . . .

Nor can a man properly be said to save anything, if he only lays it up. You may as well throw your money into the sea, as bury it in the earth. And you may as well bury it in the earth, as in your chest or in the Bank of England. Not to use, is effectually to throw it away. . . .

When the possessor of Heaven and earth brought you into being and placed you in this world, he placed you here not as a proprietor but a steward.

THE USE OF MONEY

24

I go calmly and quietly on my way, doing what I conceive to be the will of God. I do not, will not concern myself with what will be done when I am dead.

TO THOS TAYLOR, 1786

What can I advise you to in this trying hour? I would really advise you to sit still for a little while.

TO ALEXANDER CLARK, 1777

I do not remember to have heard or read anything like my own experience. Almost ever since I can remember I have been led in a peculiar way. I go on in an even line, being very little raised at one time or depressed at another. . . . I am very rarely led by impressions, but generally by reason and Scripture.

TO ELIZABETH RITCHIE, 1786

25

This was a day full of work, but, blessed be God, not tiresome work. I began in the Foundery at four, the service at West Street began at nine. In the afternoon I met the children at three, preached at five, and then had a comfortable season with the Society.

JOURNAL, 25th DECEMBER 1770

Our service began at four, as usual, in the new Chapel. I expected Mr Richardson to read prayers at West Street Chapel, but he did not come; so I read prayers myself and preached, and administered the Sacrament to several hundred people. In the afternoon I preached at the new Chapel, thoroughly filled in every corner; and in the evening at St Sepulchre's, one of the largest parish churches in London. It was warm enough, being sufficiently filled. Yet I felt no weakness or weariness, but was stronger after I had preached my fourth sermon than I was after the first.

JOURNAL, 25th DECEMBER, 1778

26

I am never tired in my work. From the beginning of the day or the week or the year to the end I do not know what weariness means. I am never weary of writing or preaching or travelling; but am just as fresh at the end as at the beginning.

TO JAMES BARRY, 1784

I am never so busy as not spare a little time to remember my friends.

TO RICHARD WHATCOAT, 1788

I am ashamed of my indolence and inactivity. The good Lord help us both!

TO CHARLES WESLEY, 1772

27

I beseech you by the mercies of God that you never avail yourselves of the Deed of Declaration to assume any superiority over your brethren, but let all things go on among those Itinerants who choose to remain together, exactly in the same manner as when I was with you, so far as circumstances permit.

In particular, I beseech you, if you ever loved me and if you now love God and your brethren, to have no respect of persons in stationing the preachers, in choosing children for Kingswood School, in disposing of the yearly contribution and the Preachers' Fund or any other public money. But do all things with a single eye, as I have done from the beginning. Go on thus, doing all things without prejudice or partiality, and God will be with you even to the end.

TO THE METHODIST CONFERENCE, 1785[1]

28

The Conference have unanimously resolved that all the preachers who are in full connexion with them shall enjoy every privilege that the members of the Conference enjoy, agreeably to the above-written letter of our venerable deceased father in the Gospel.

[1]To be opened and read after his death.

It may be expected that the Conference make some observations on the death of Mr Wesley; but they find themselves utterly inadequate to express their ideas and feelings on this awful and affecting event.

Their souls do truly mourn for their great loss; and they trust they shall give the most substantial proofs of their veneration for the memory of their most esteemed father and friend by endeavouring with great humility and diffidence to follow and imitate him in doctrine, discipline and life.

RESOLUTION OF METHODIST CONFERENCE FOLLOWING
WESLEY'S DEATH

29

Unless the Divine power has raised you up to be as *Athanasius contra mundum,* I see not how you can go through your glorious enterprise in opposing that execrable villainy, which is the scandal of religion, of England, and of human nature. Unless God has raised you up for this very purpose, you will be worn out by the opposition of men and devils. But if God be for you, who can be against you? O be not weary of well doing! Go on, in the name of God, and in the power of His might, till even American slavery (the vilest that ever saw the sun) shall vanish away before it.

Reading this morning a tract wrote by a poor African, I was particularly struck by that circumstance, that a man who has a black skin, being wronged or outraged by a white man, can have no redress; it being a *law* in all our Colonies that the *oath* of a black against a white goes for nothing. What villainy is this!

That He who has guided you from youth up may continue to strengthen you in this and all things is the prayer of, dear sir, John Wesley.

TO WM WILBERFORCE 1791[1]

[1] Wesleys last letter.

30

I give six pounds to be divided among the six poor men who shall carry my body to the grave; for I particularly desire that there may be no hearse, no coach, no escutcheon, no pomp, except the tears of them that loved me, and are following me to Abraham's bosom. I solemnly adjure my Executors, in the name of God, punctually to observe this.

LAST WILL AND TESTAMENT, 1789

31

Forsake me not, when my strength faileth.

.   .   .   .   .

How necessary it is for everyone to be on the right foundation!

.   .   .   .   .

There is no way into the holiest but by the blood of Jesus.

.   .   .   .   .

The best of all is, God is with us.
It is the Lord's doing, and marvellous in our eyes.

.   .   .   .   .

He giveth his servants rest.

.   .   .   .   .

We thank Thee, O Lord, for these and all Thy mercies; bless the Church and King, and grant us truth and peace, through Jesus Christ our Lord, for ever and ever.

LAST WORDS